Coloring The Blended Family

Coloring With Kindness

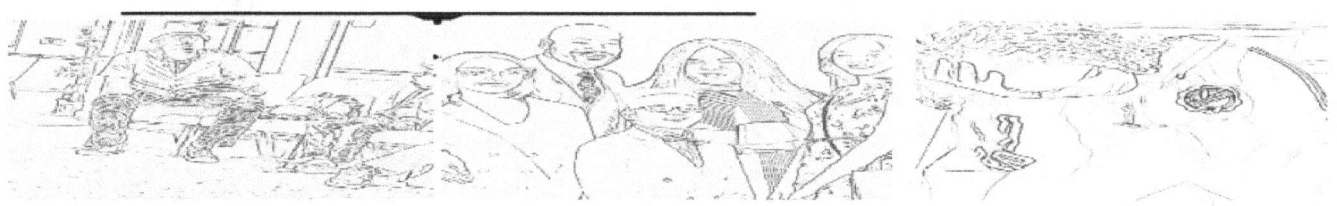

Coloring The Blended Family
Richard Patterson III

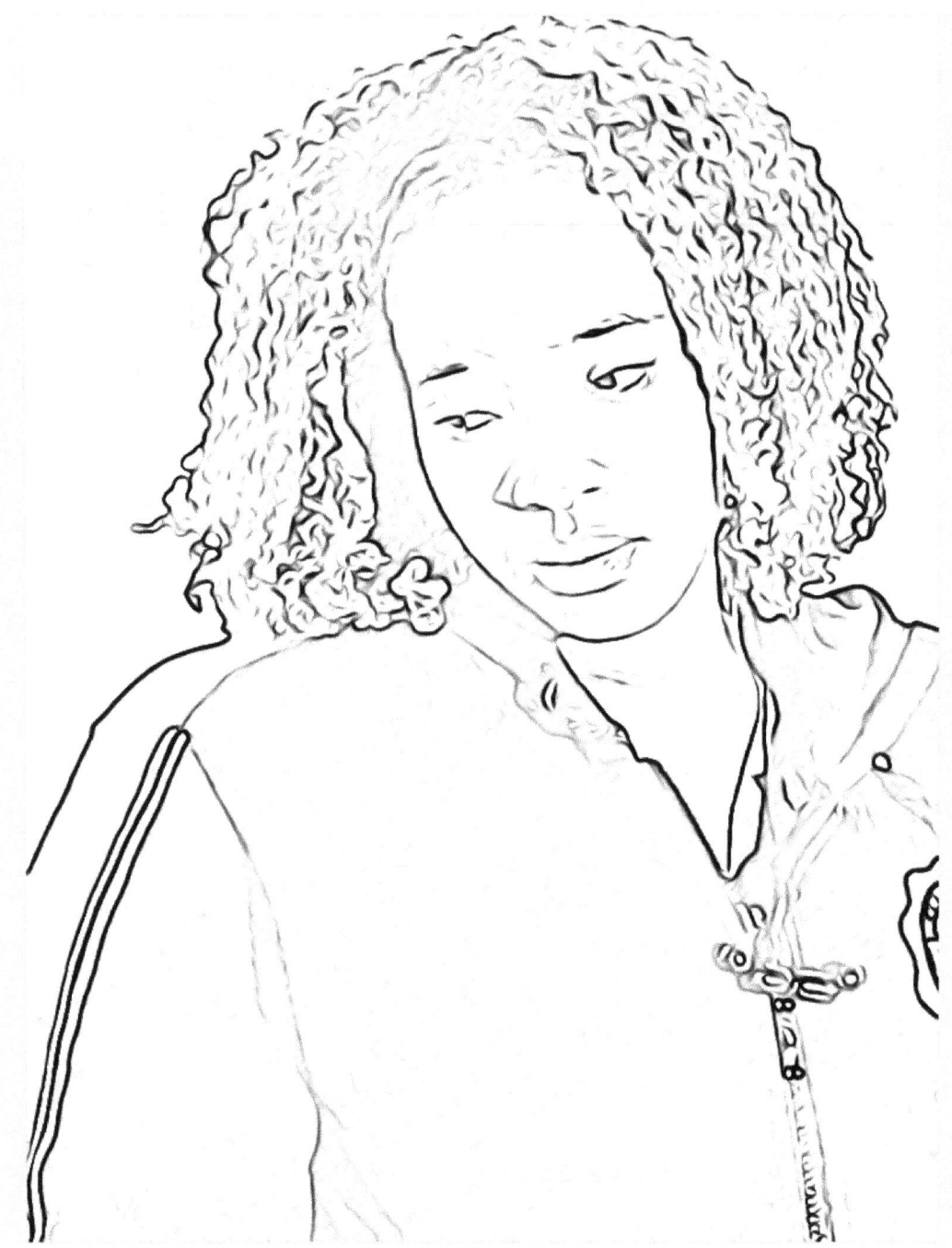

Are you a single parent? If so chances are you have to interact with the child's other side of the family. None of us raise children the same way so we are all trying to blend understanding what family looks like for us.

Coloring With Kindness , Page 2

Coloring The Blended Family
Richard Patterson III

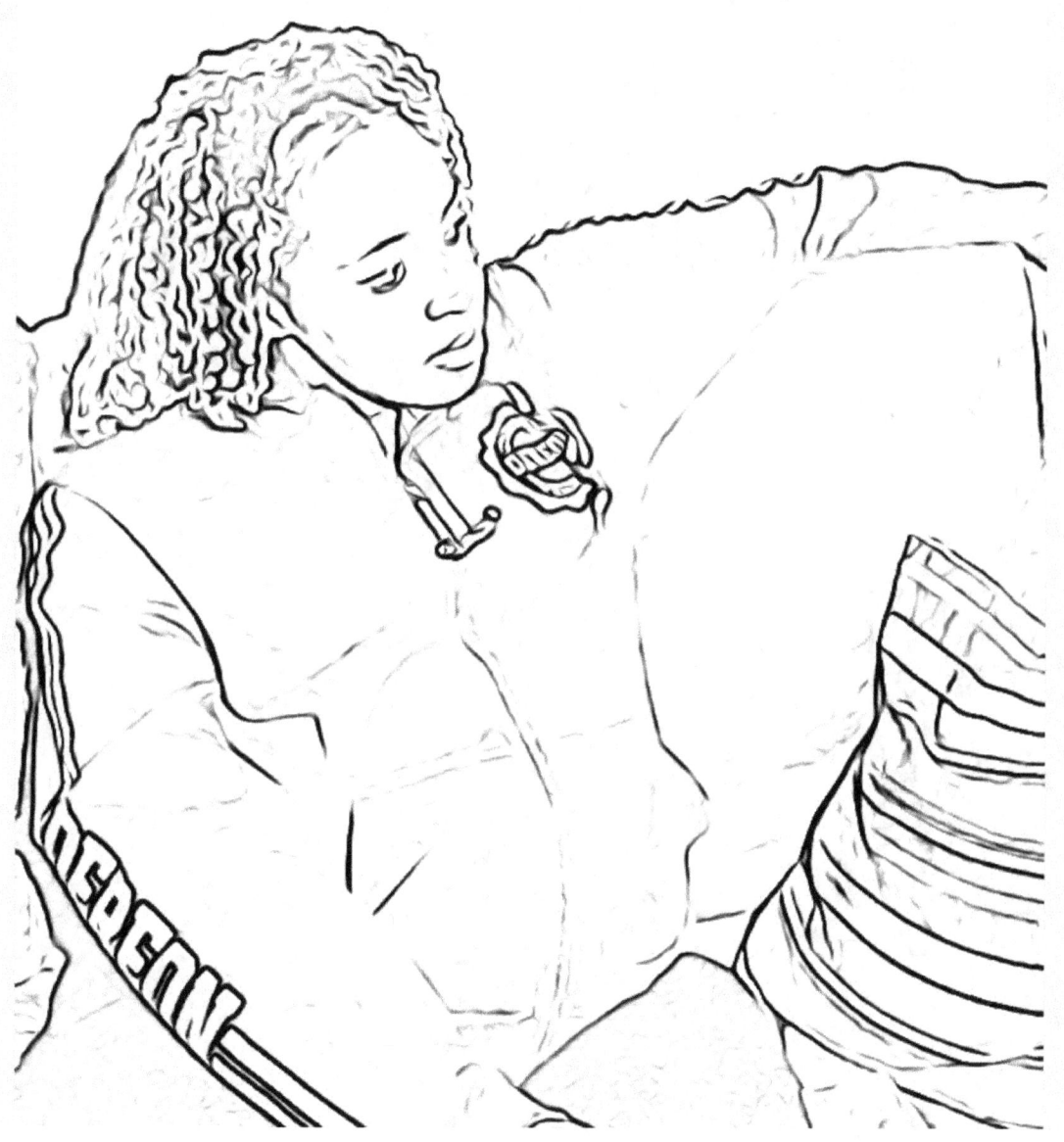

After you get off work it would be ideal to sit and relax, but most single parent households don't have this courtesy. With cheer practices and homework, help is a necessity.

Coloring The Blended Family
Richard Patterson III

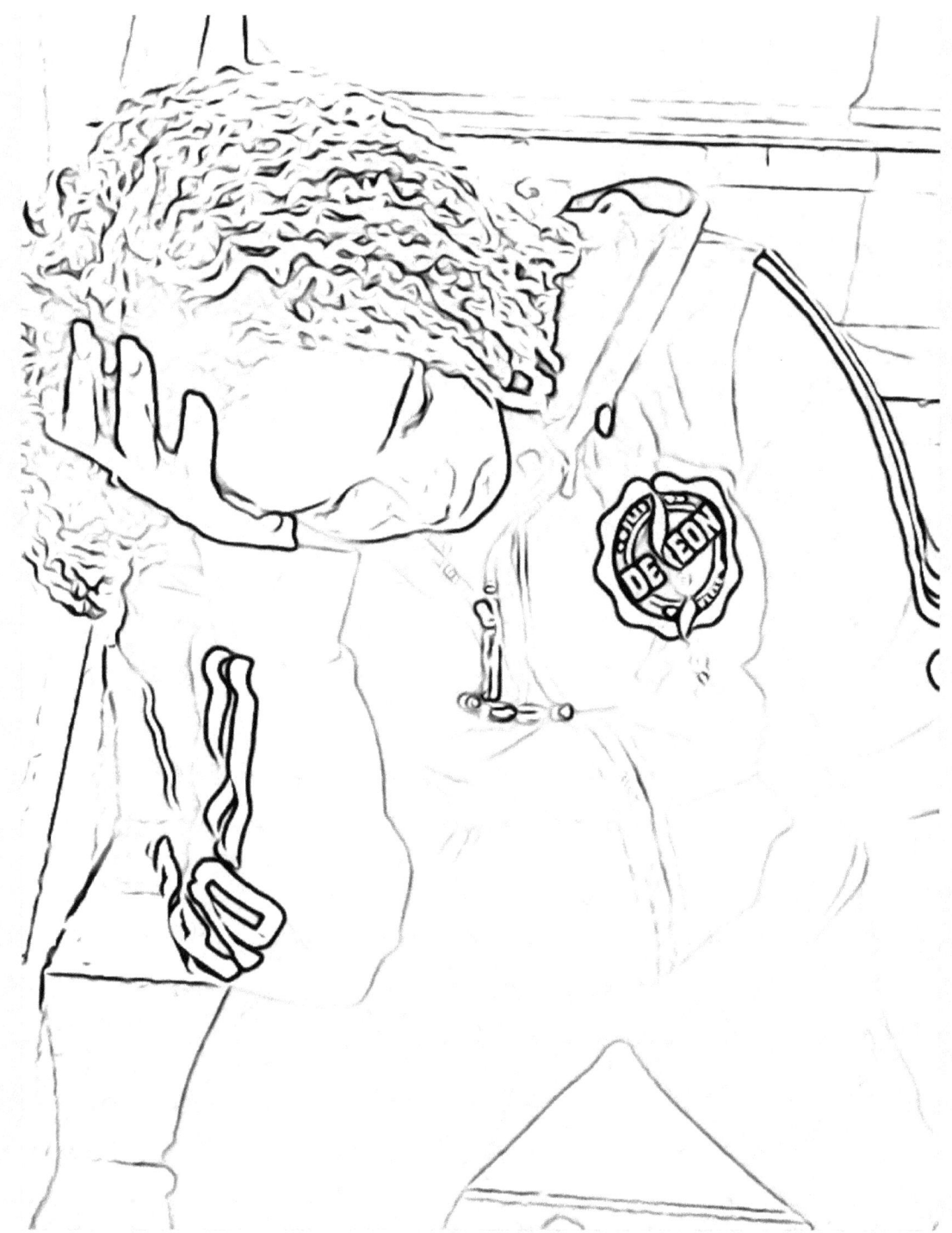

What about the bills, rent due and it seems you're robbing Peter to pay Paul all the time. Help would be nice but most times you have to negotiate things yourself to keep the house running. Where is the father? Why is it so hard?

Coloring With Kindness, Page 4

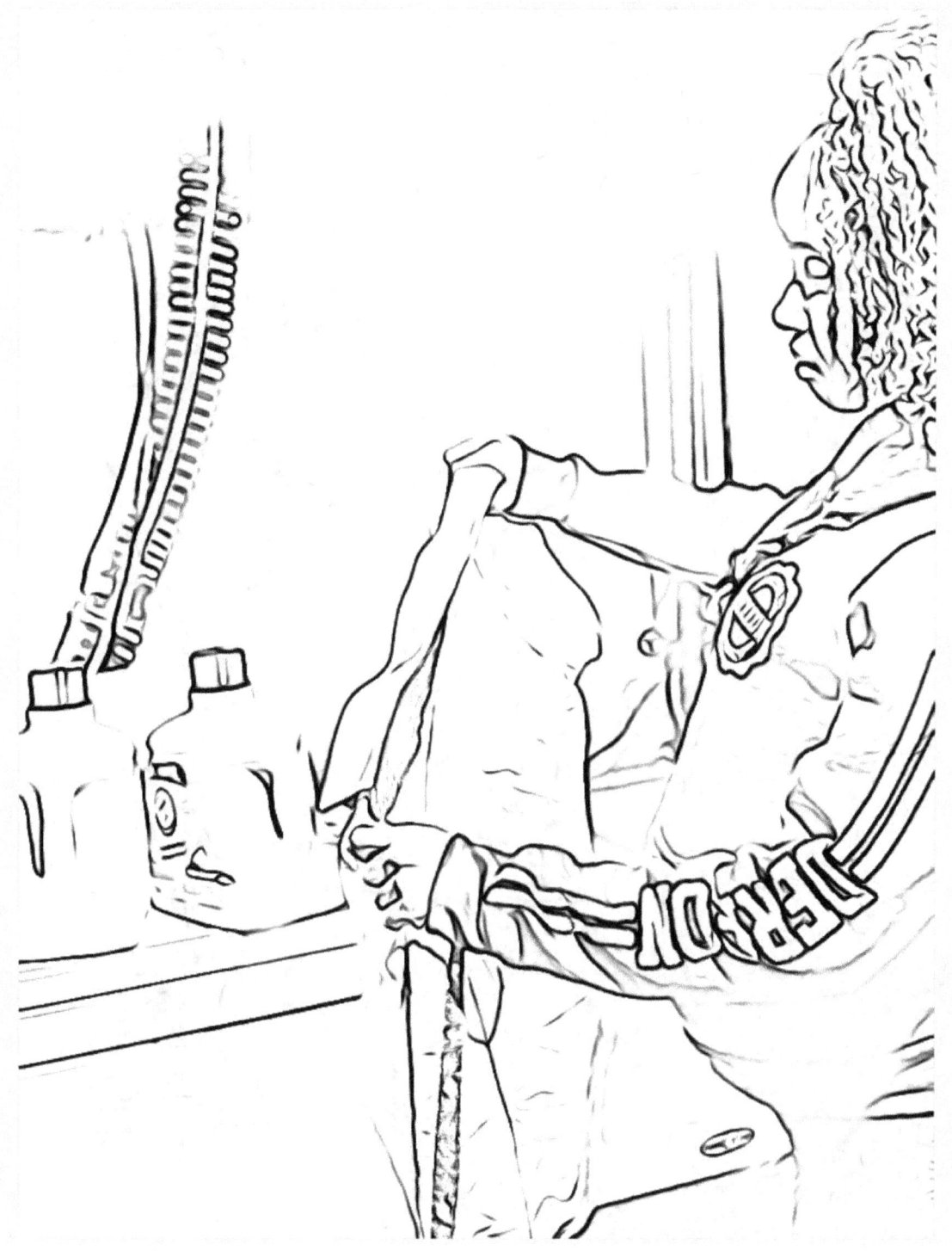

Your weeks are spent washing clothes to maintain the order. Only to turn around and do the exact same thing next week. There has to be more to life than this.

Coloring The Blended Family
Richard Patterson III

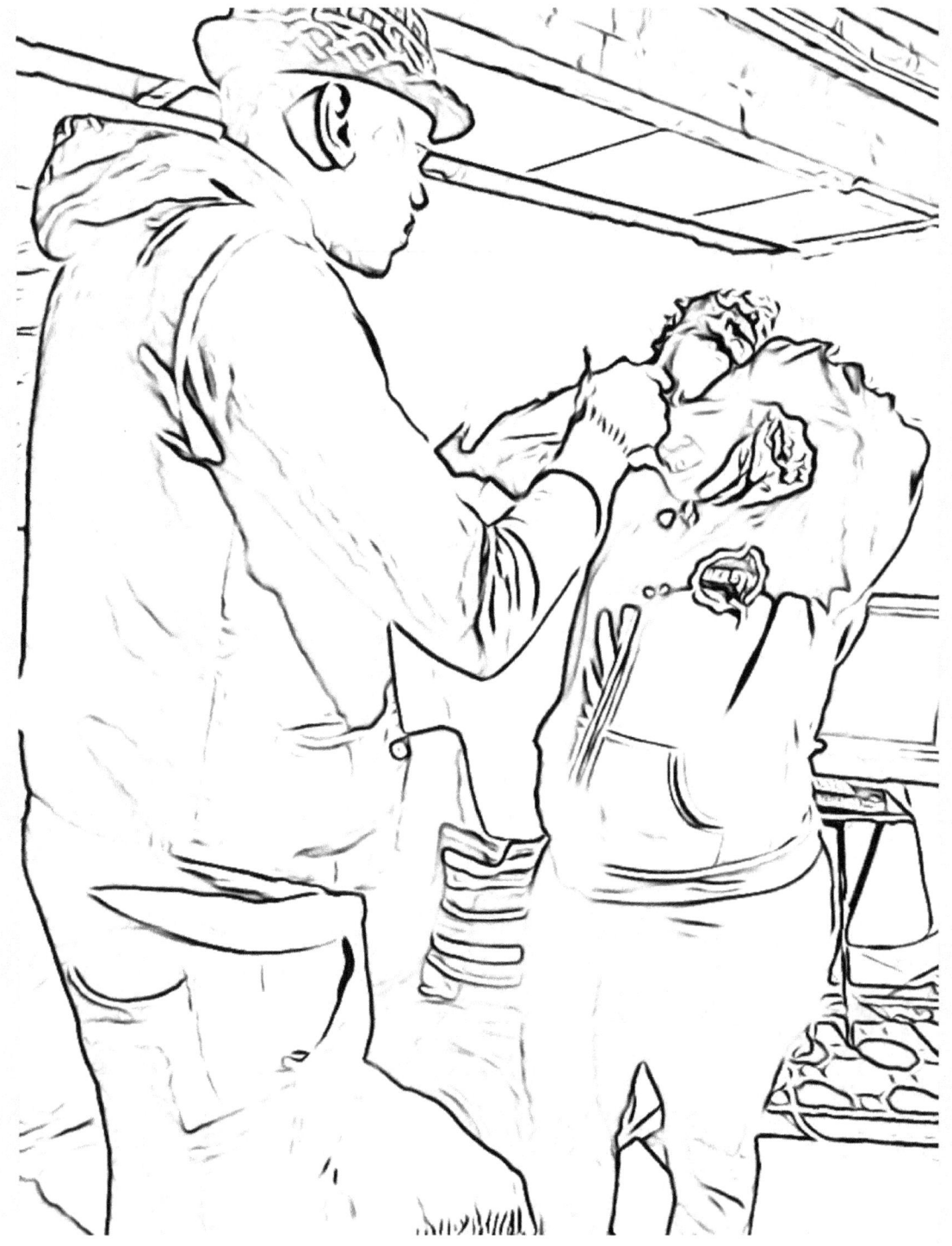

It seems as if anytime you have a conversation with your child's father it ends up being some type of conflict. Why can't we just come to an agreement on how to raise the child and get rid of all the other animosity?

Coloring With Kindness , Page 6

Coloring The Blended Family
Richard Patterson III

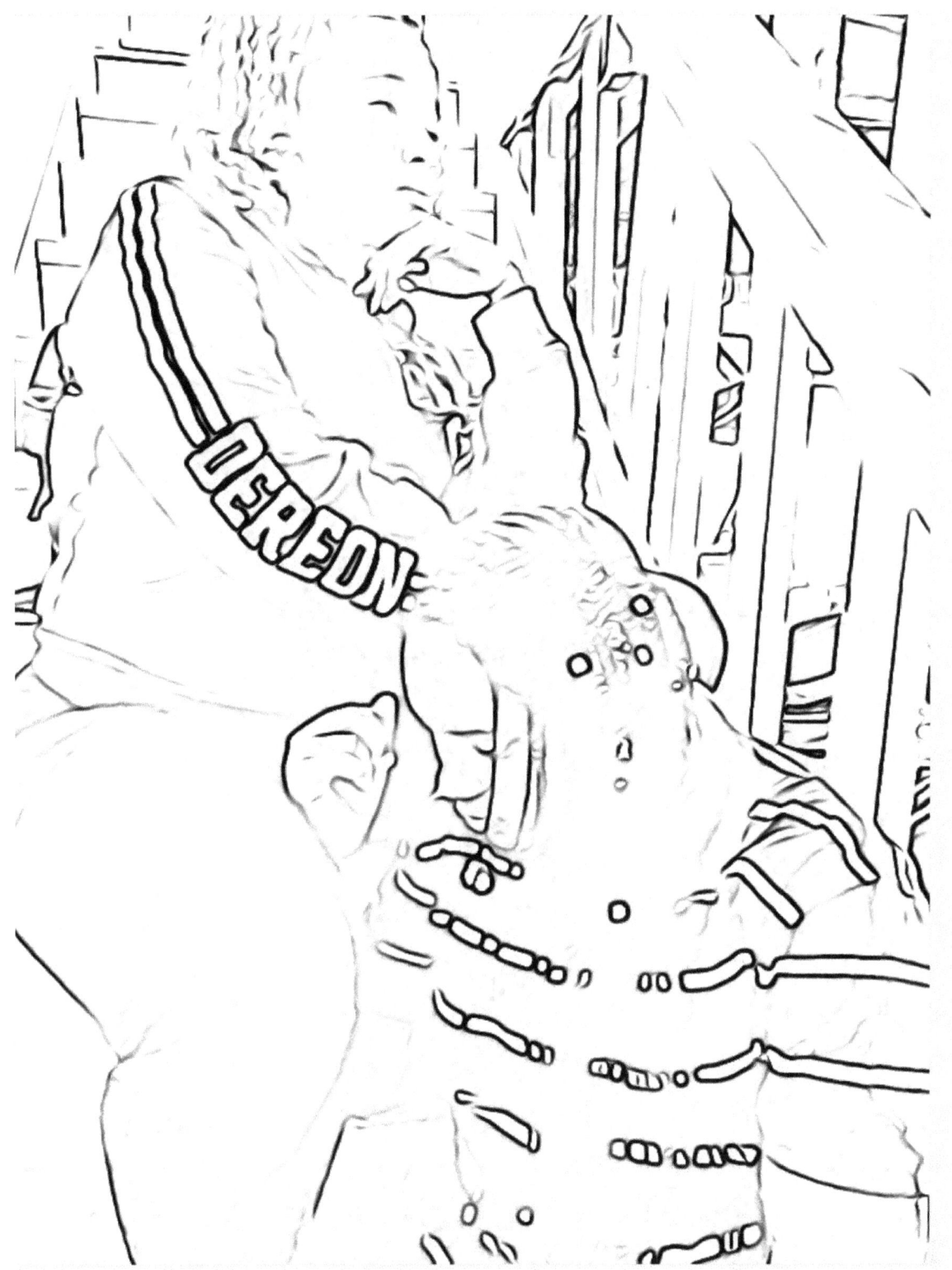

You are tired of explaining to your child why things are so stressful.
How do I create an environment where my child can flourish?

Coloring With Kindness , Page 7

Coloring The Blended Family
Richard Patterson III

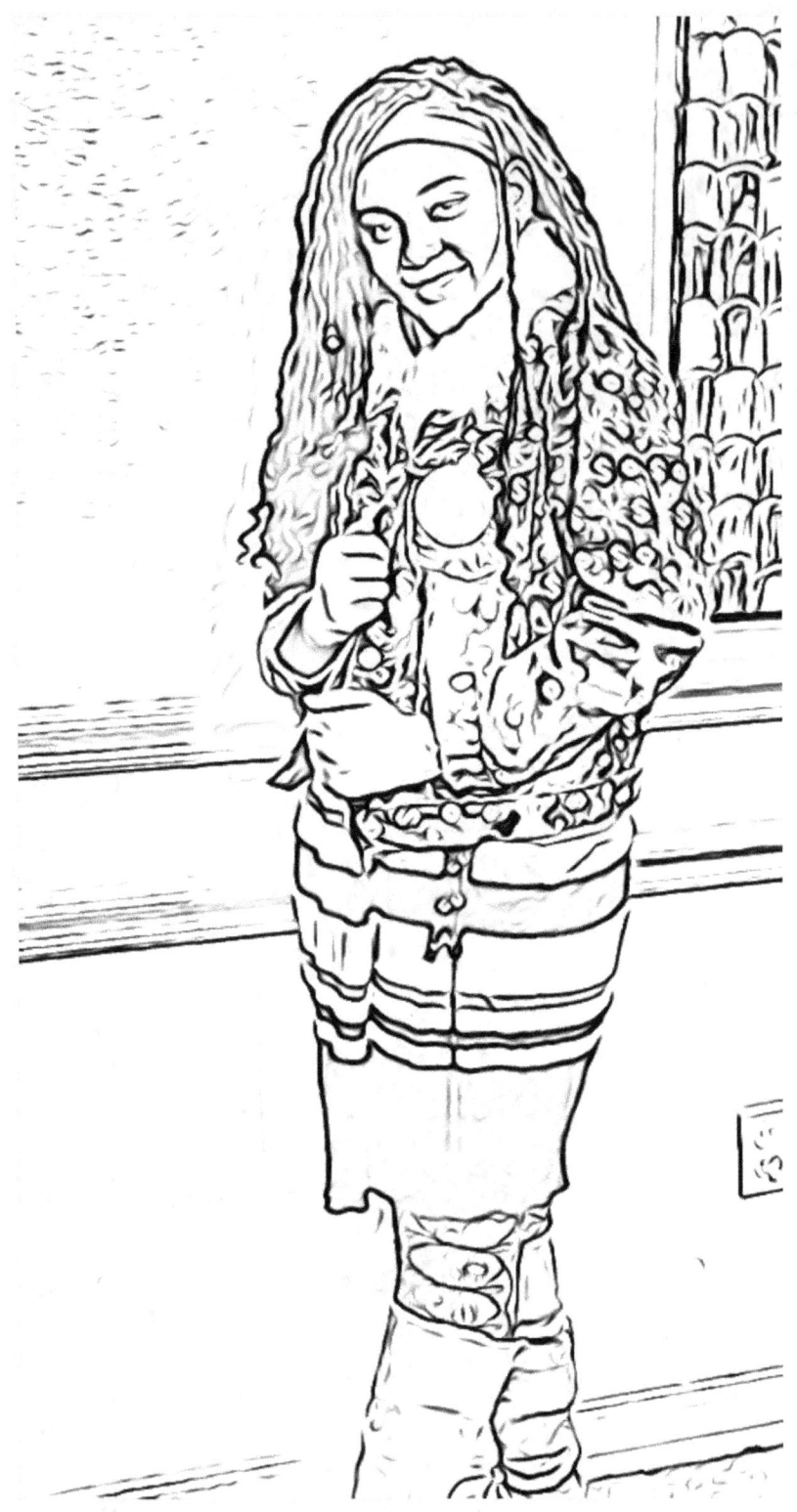

The only thing that keeps you going is that beautiful smile you see everyday. You keep it together for your child and make the best of your situation.

Coloring The Blended Family
Richard Patterson III

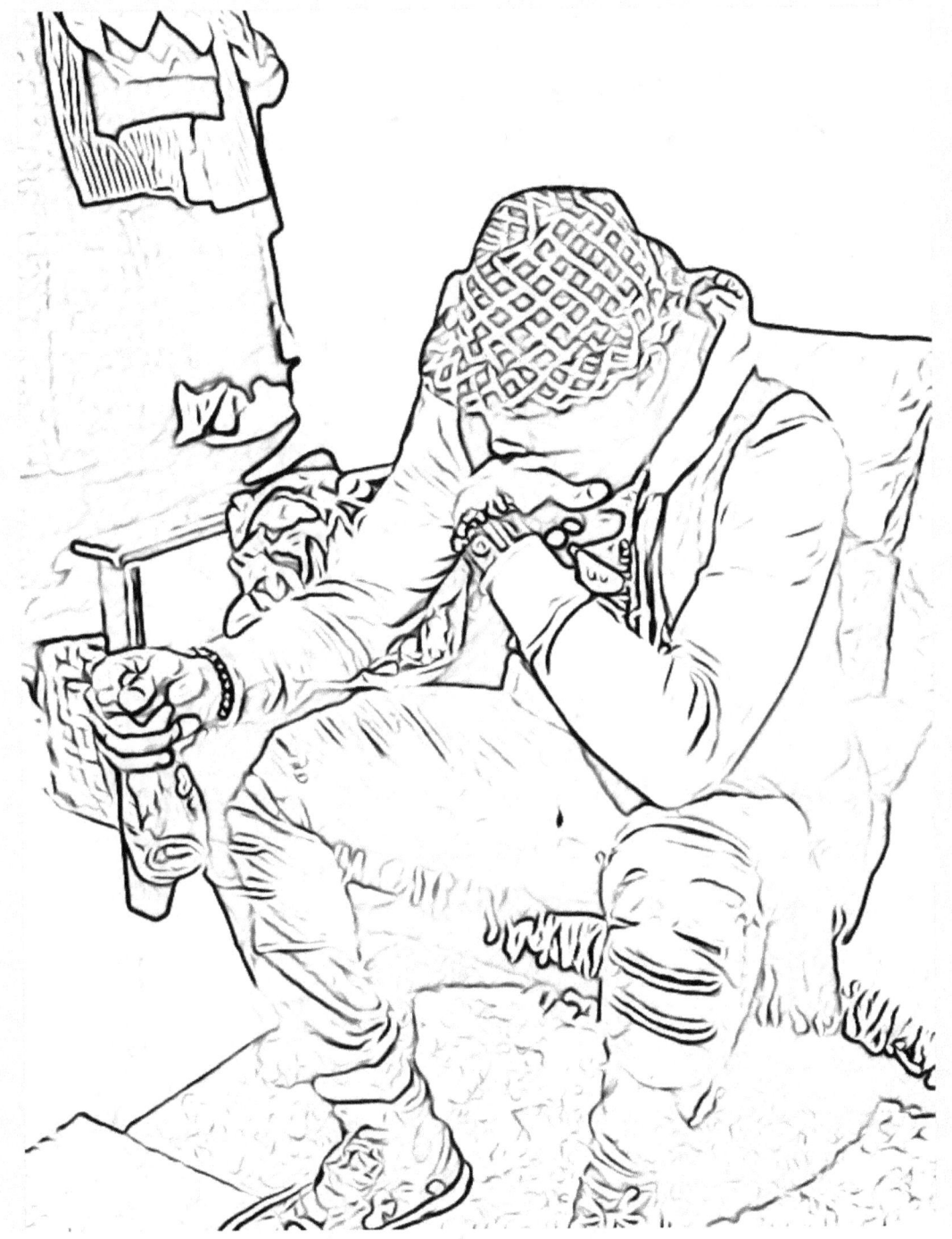

Are you a single father? The perspective if you're not paying child support is that some are dead beats. In some cases the father is dead broke (not a dead beat). I have children from my Ex-wife and now another woman who I'm not with.

Coloring The Blended Family
Richard Patterson III

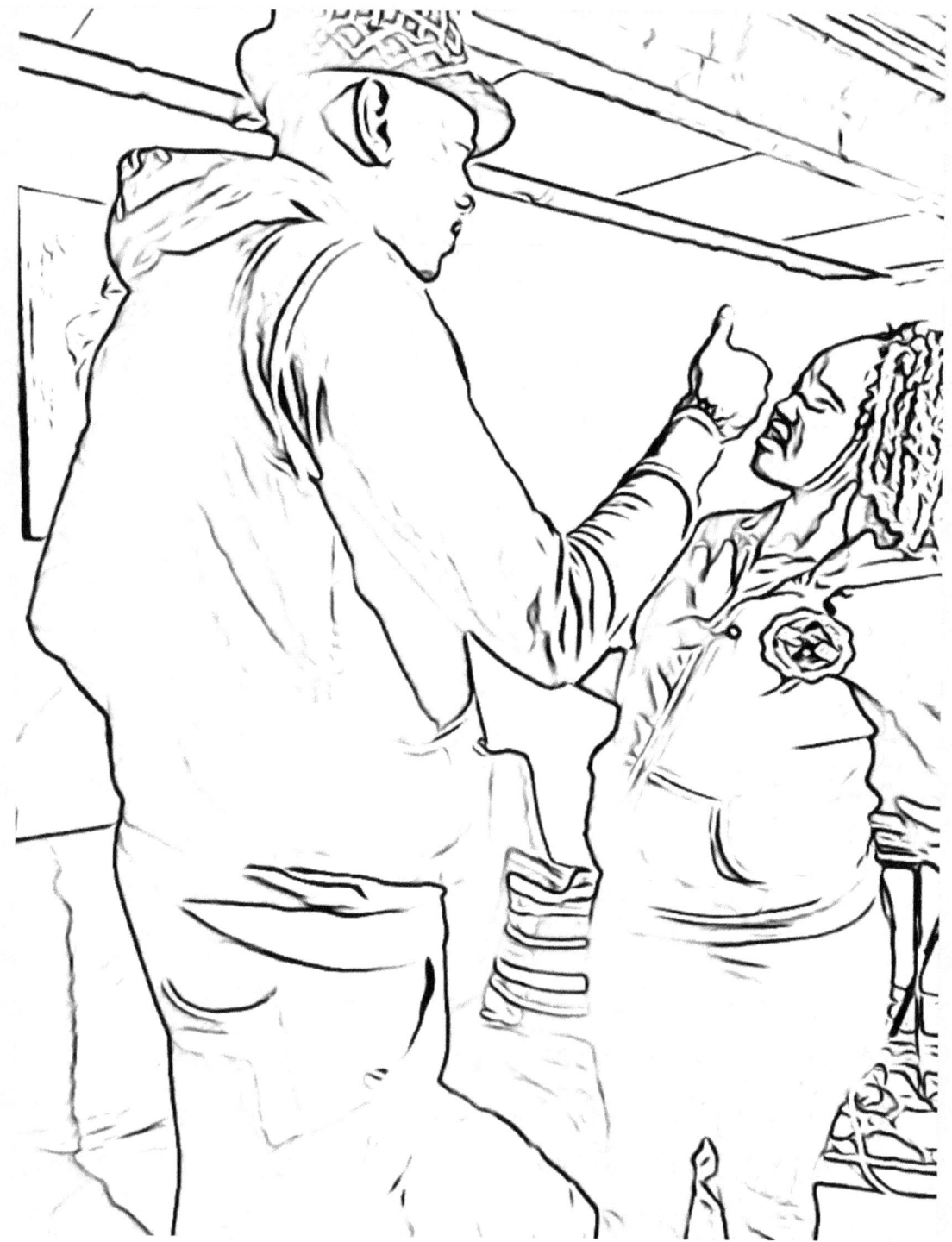

The mother is talking to me about money but can't you see I'm trying. I'm working so much I barely get to see my children, plus I feel like no progress is being made in my life so at times I'm angry too.

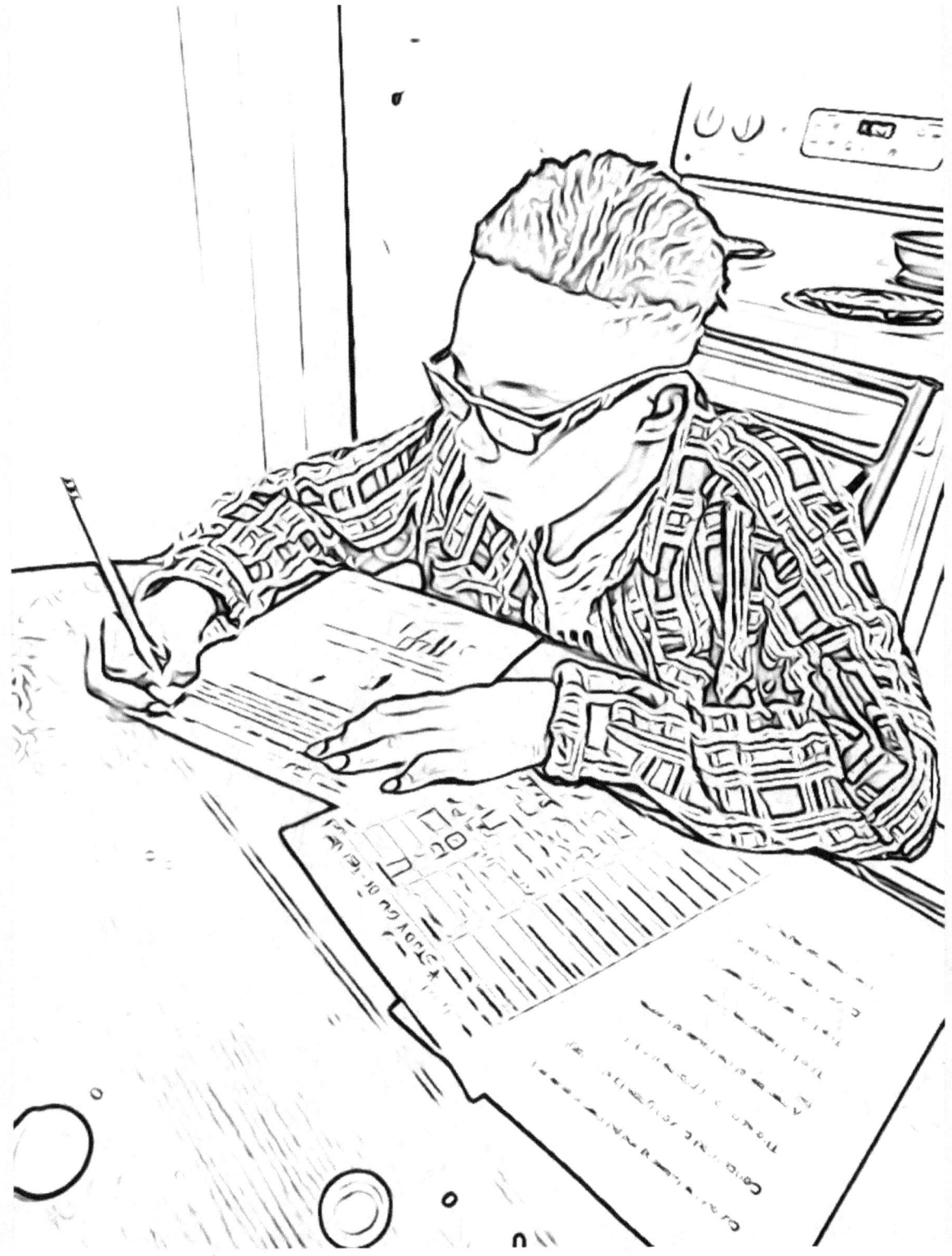

In everything that we deal with on a day to day basis. Here's this child that's innocent and needs to be raised effectively as possible.

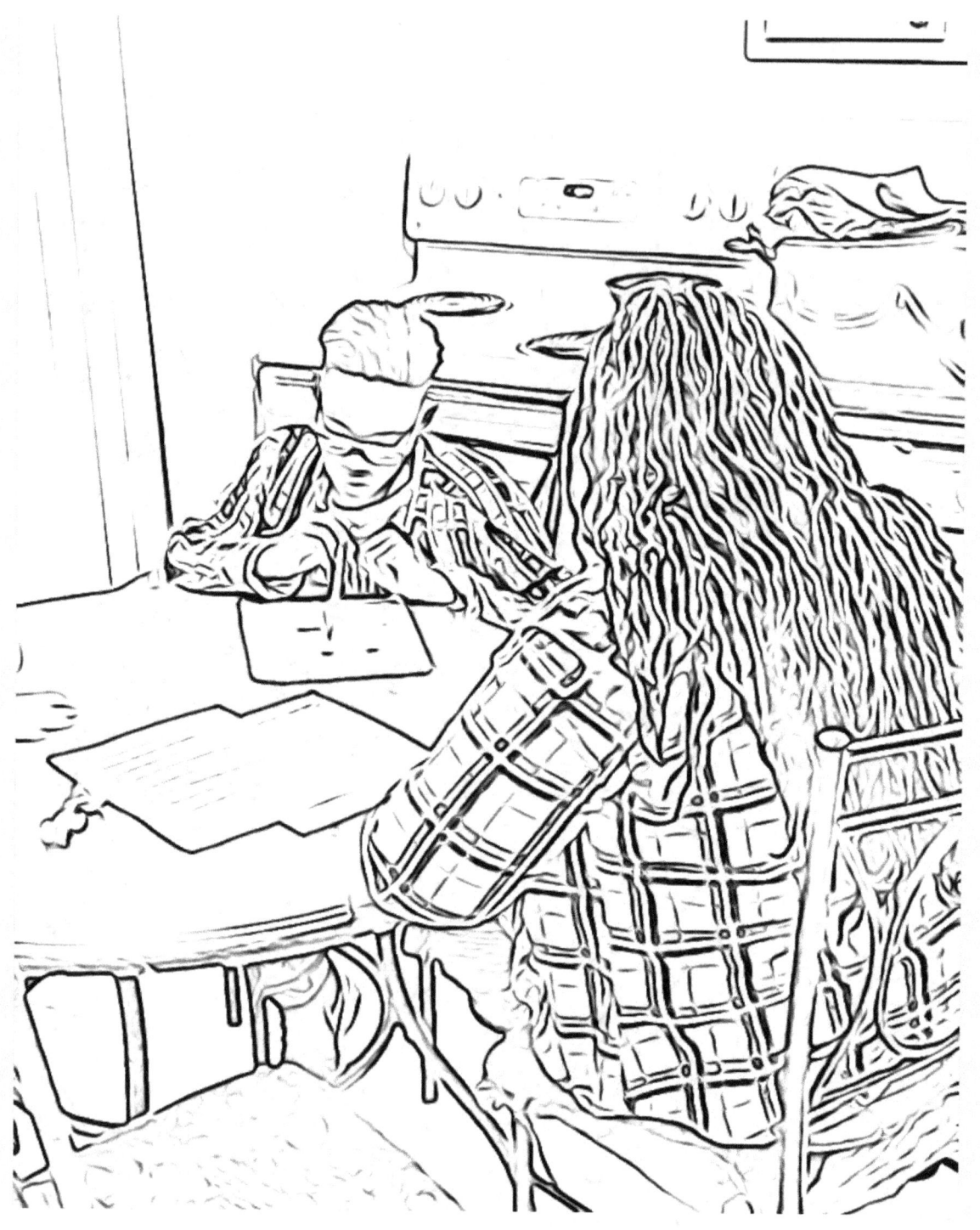

Are you a two parent home? Both Mom & Dad but it seems like you still need another set of hands because there's not enough time in the day. 6am leaving the home by 7pm eating dinner, and by 9pm preparing for the next day

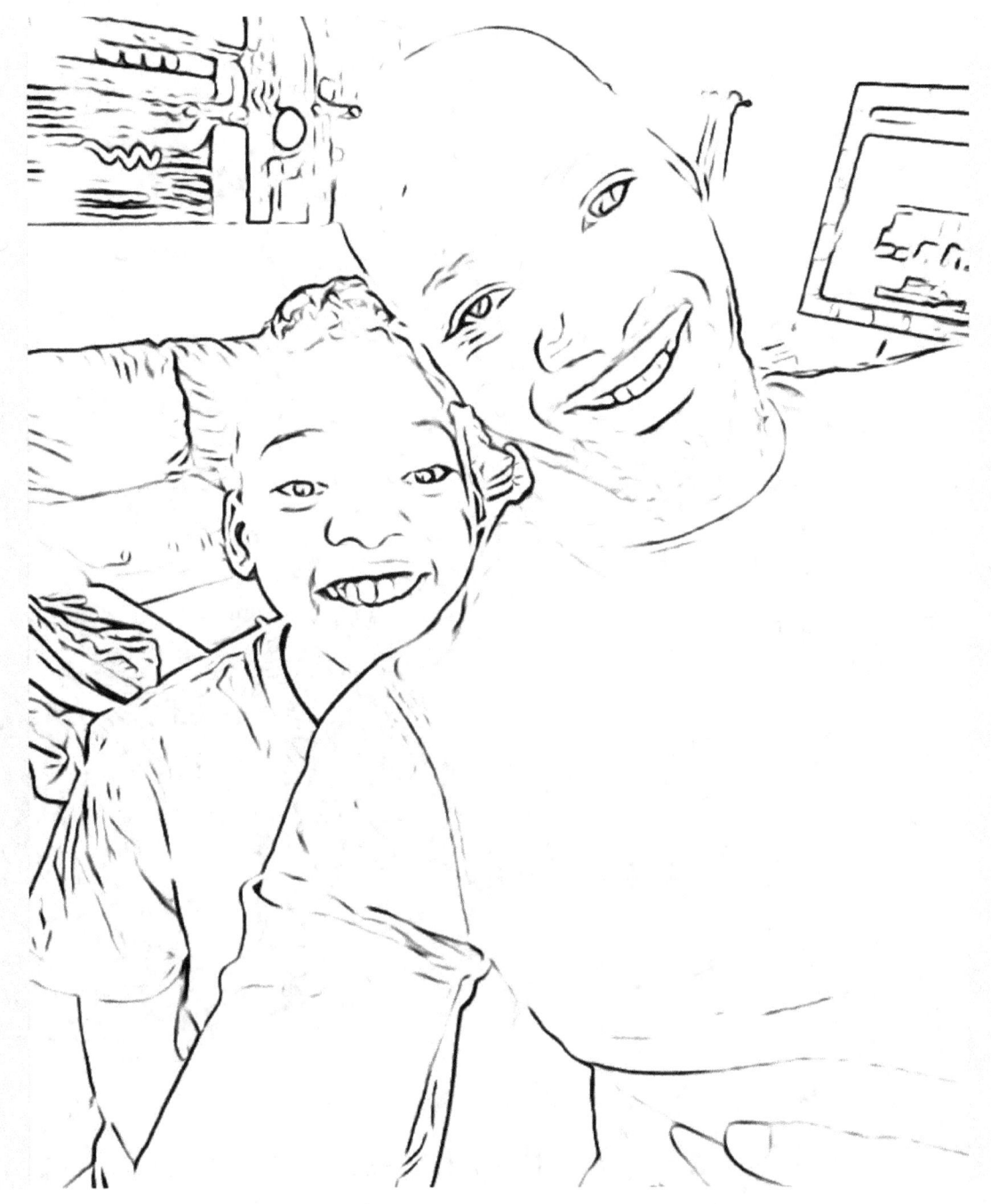

What makes a good father? Is it the money alone. Fathers across this country love their children and a lot of them spend time with their children. Being a father is being available with your time, counsel and resources.

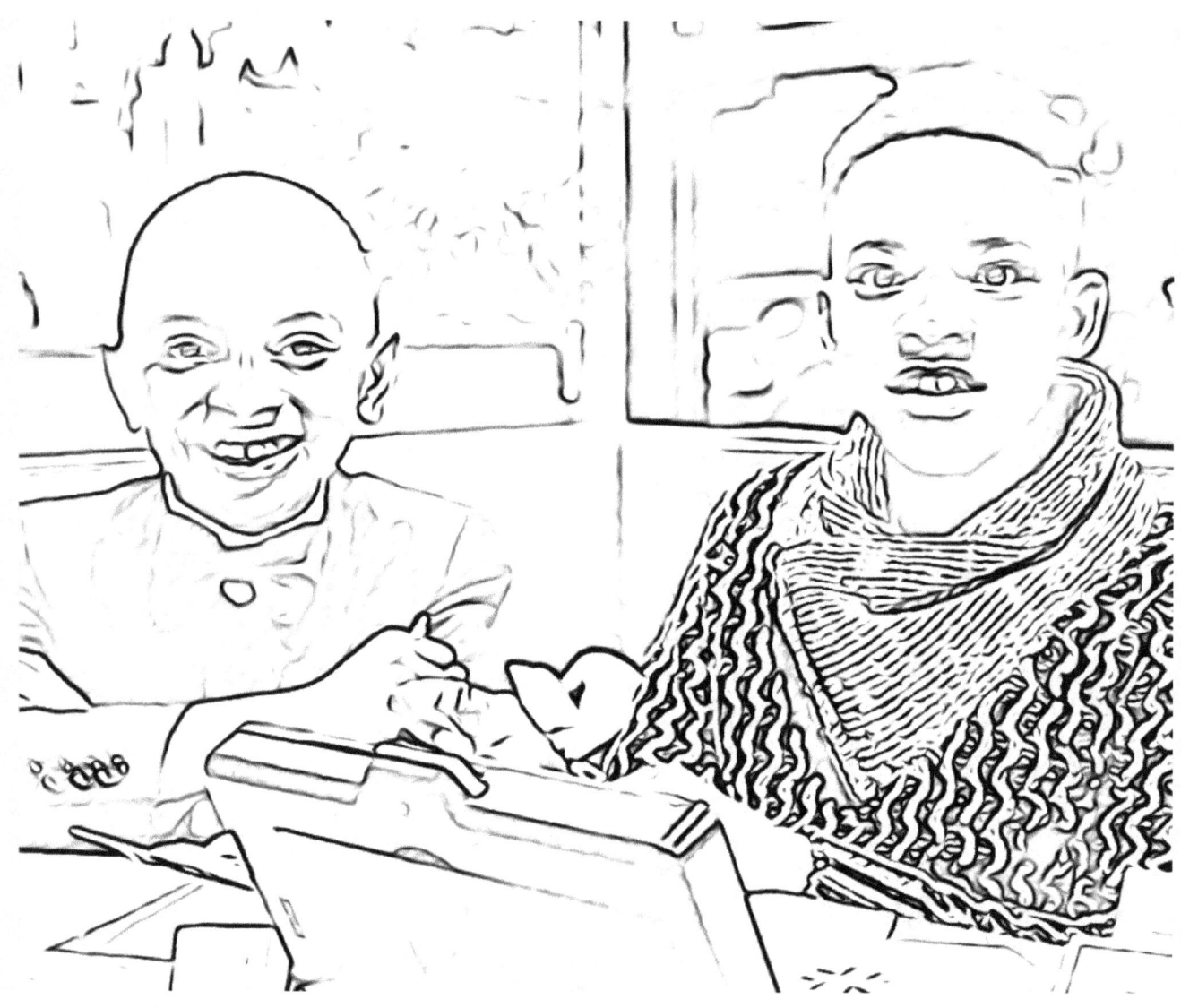

The same father or mother doesn't make us a family, but the love we have for one another Blends us together as one family.

Coloring The Blended Family
Richard Patterson III

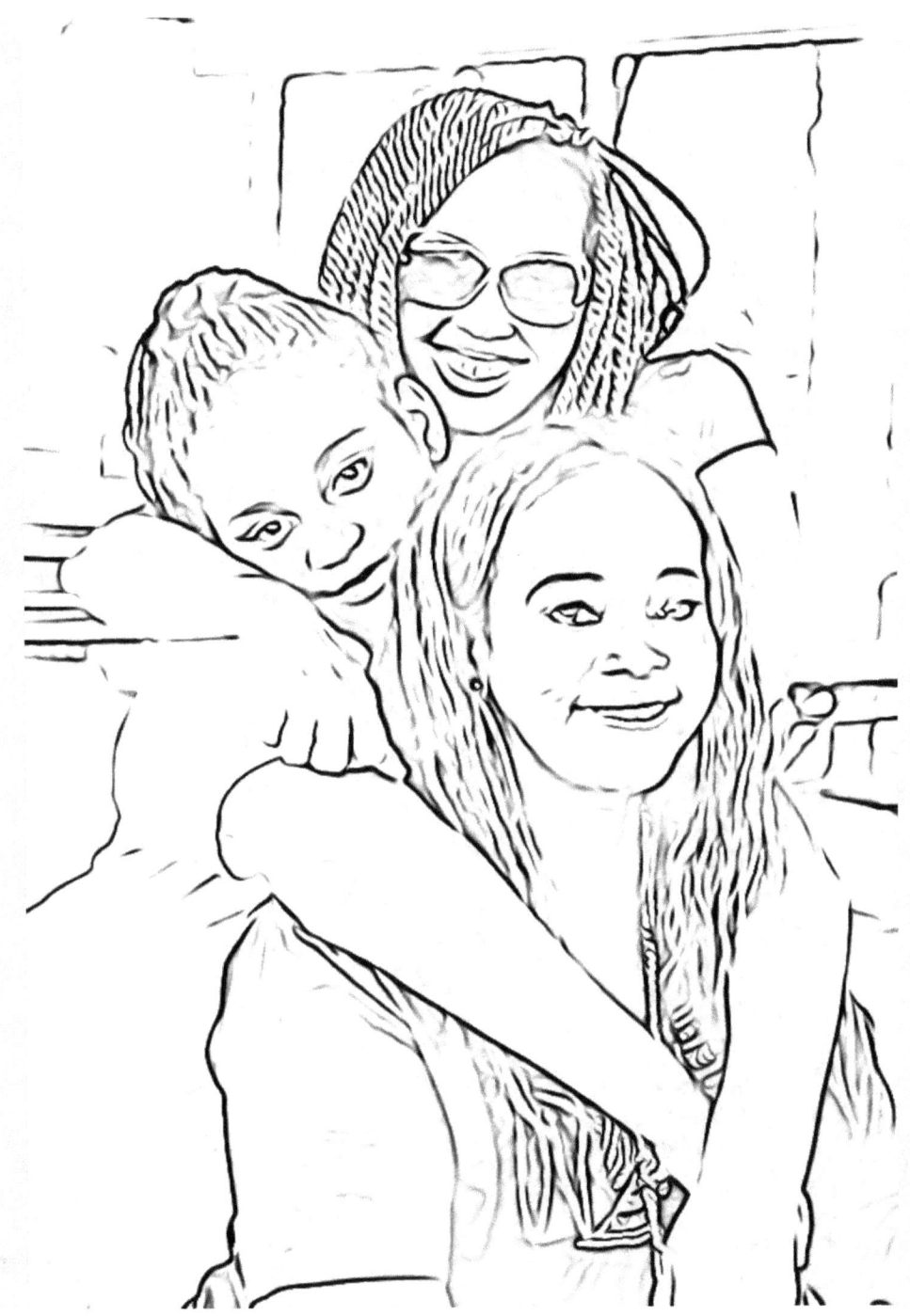

Never discount the time you spend with your children. Their view of family is being shaped during those times of leisure, recreation and everyday interactions.

Coloring The Blended Family
Richard Patterson III

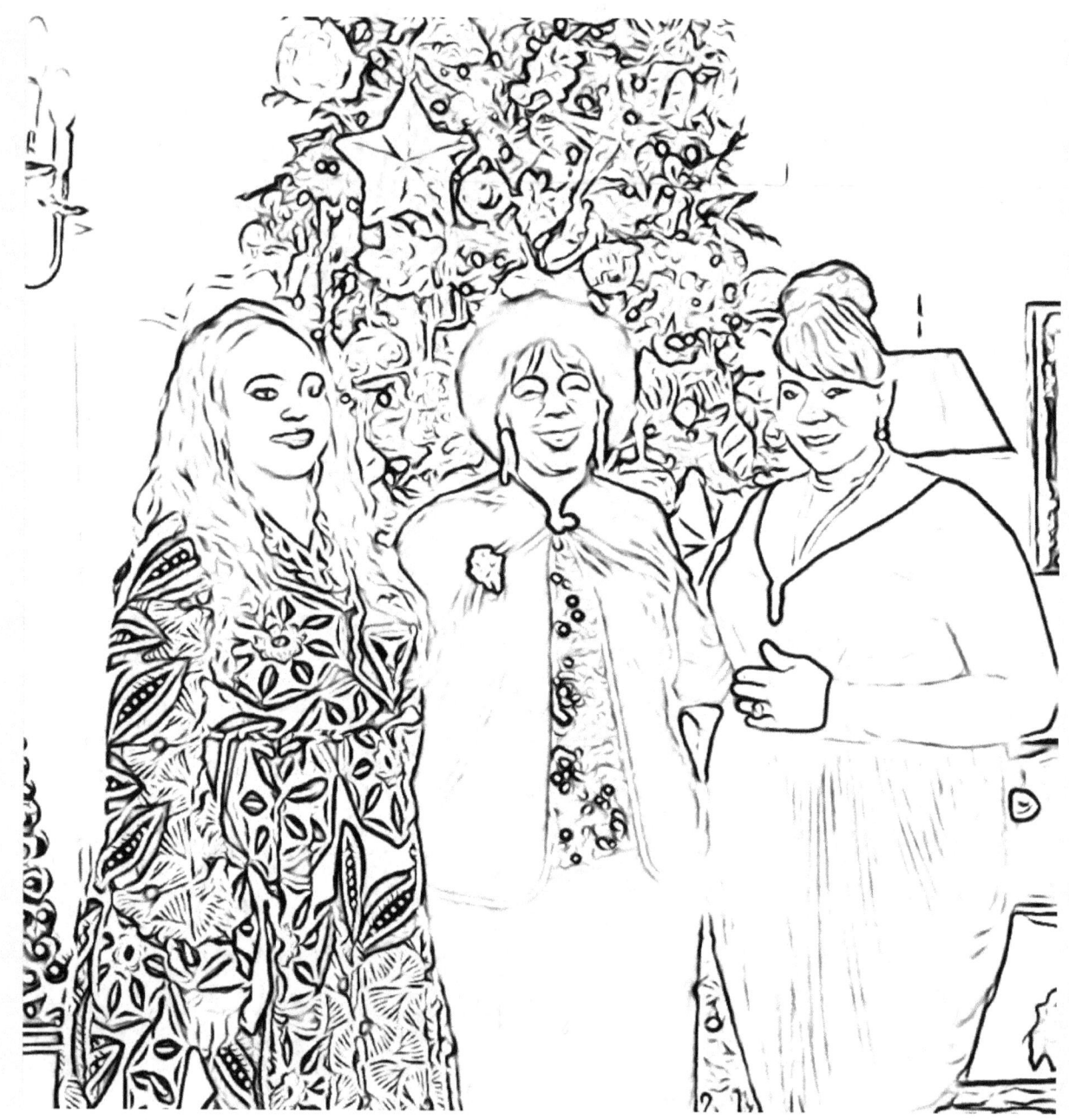

She may not be your mother but if she loves you enough to provide counsel. She's a mother figure and apart of your Blended Family.

Coloring With Kindness, Page 16

Coloring The Blended Family
Richard Patterson III

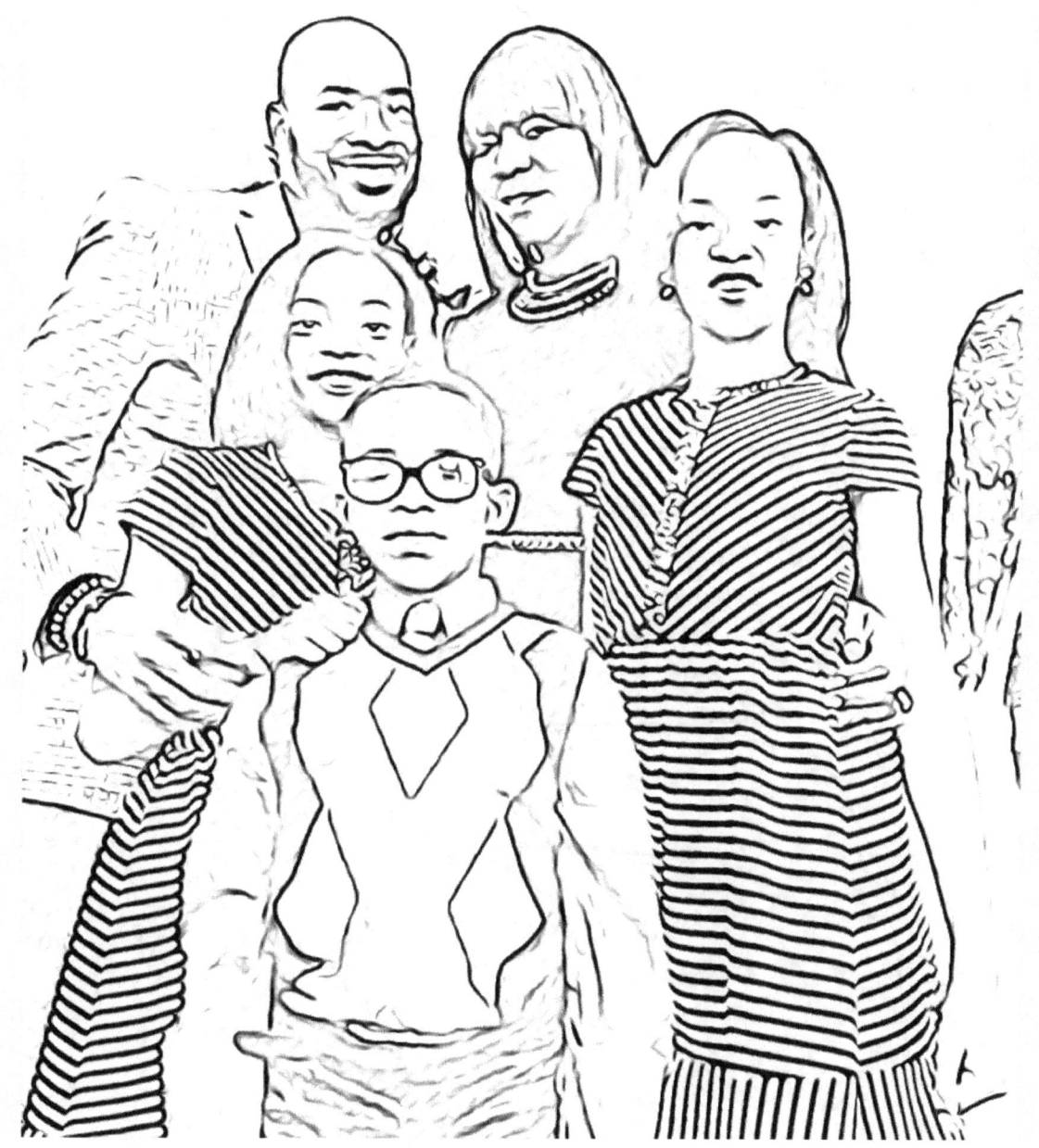

How long did it take for your family to look like this? And although it looks good what are the challenges that you've overcome or overcoming?

Coloring With Kindness , Page 17

Coloring The Blended Family
Richard Patterson III

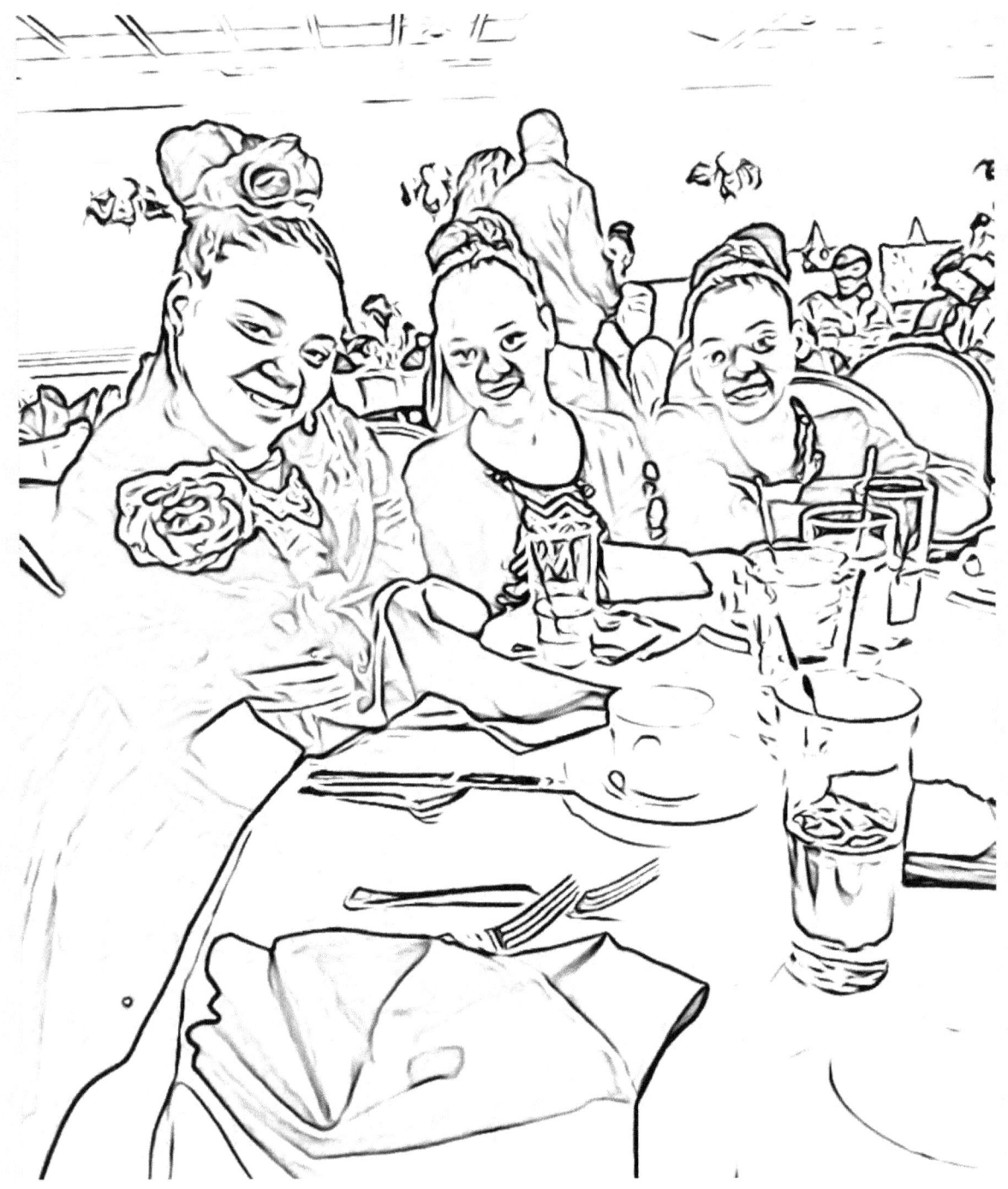

One daughter from the first marriage and two from the current one under one roof. How are you making this work?

Coloring With Kindness, Page 18

Coloring The Blended Family
Richard Patterson III

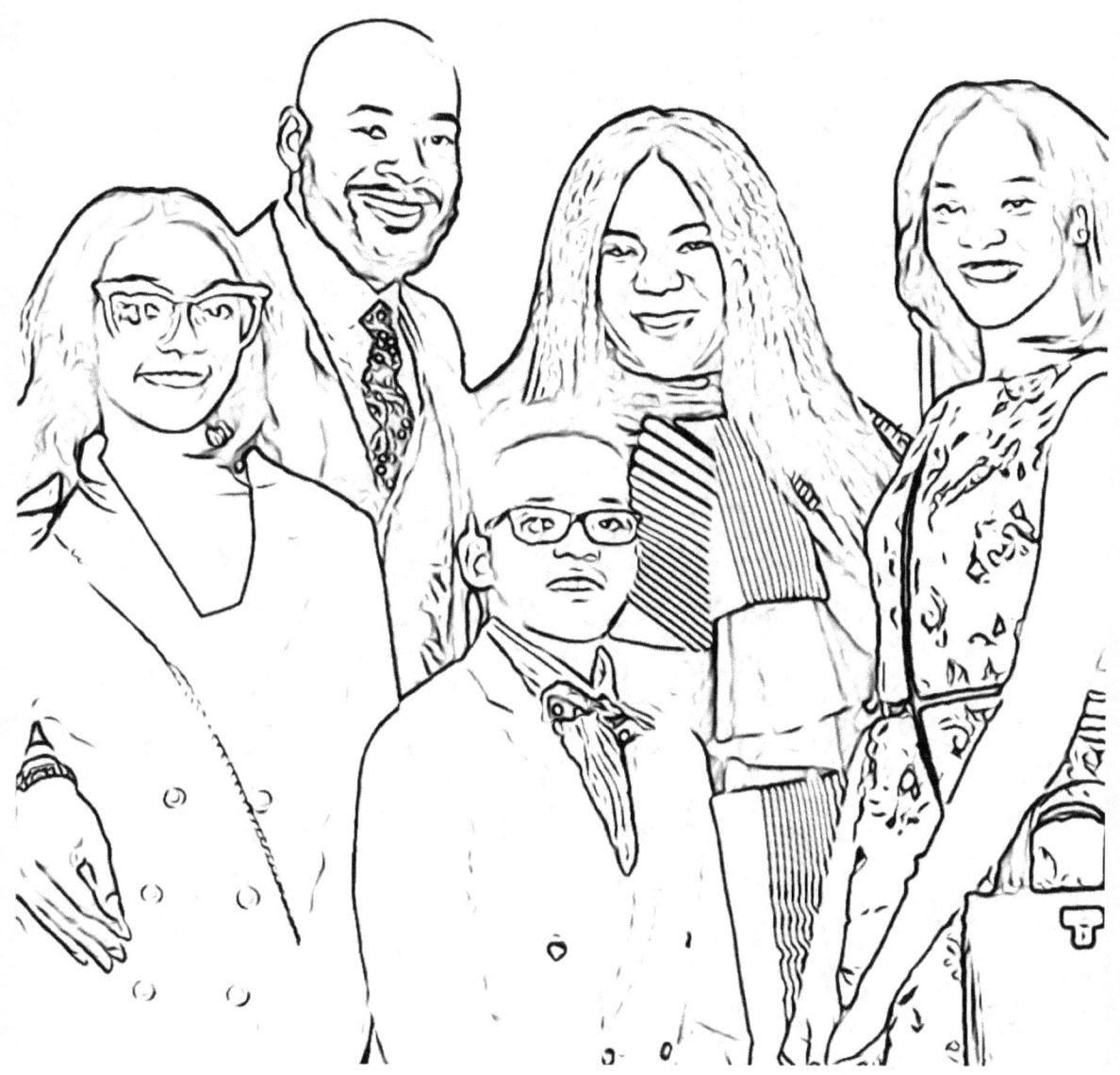

People see what looks great but always understand things are never perfect, but like a picture what makes the family great is that we all choose to stay in position. Capturing our today (Engaged with every moment) that's how we Blend the family.

Coloring With Kindness, Page 19

Coloring The Blended Family
Richard Patterson III

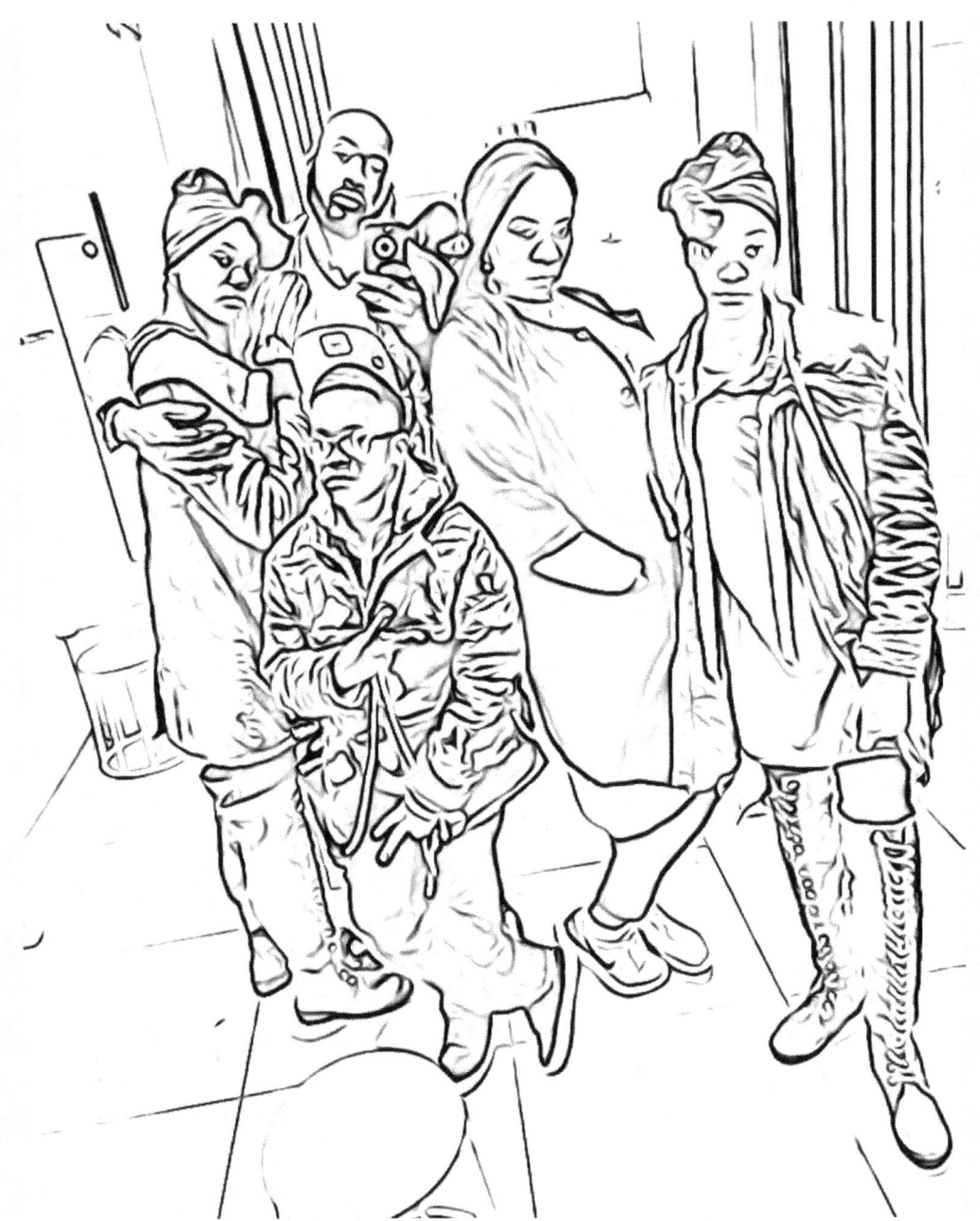

If we could sit down and talk to you, we would tell you it's been a Roller coaster ride. The real key to Coloring or somewhat defining The Blended Family is embracing the help that God sends through healthy relationships.

Coloring With Kindness , Page 20

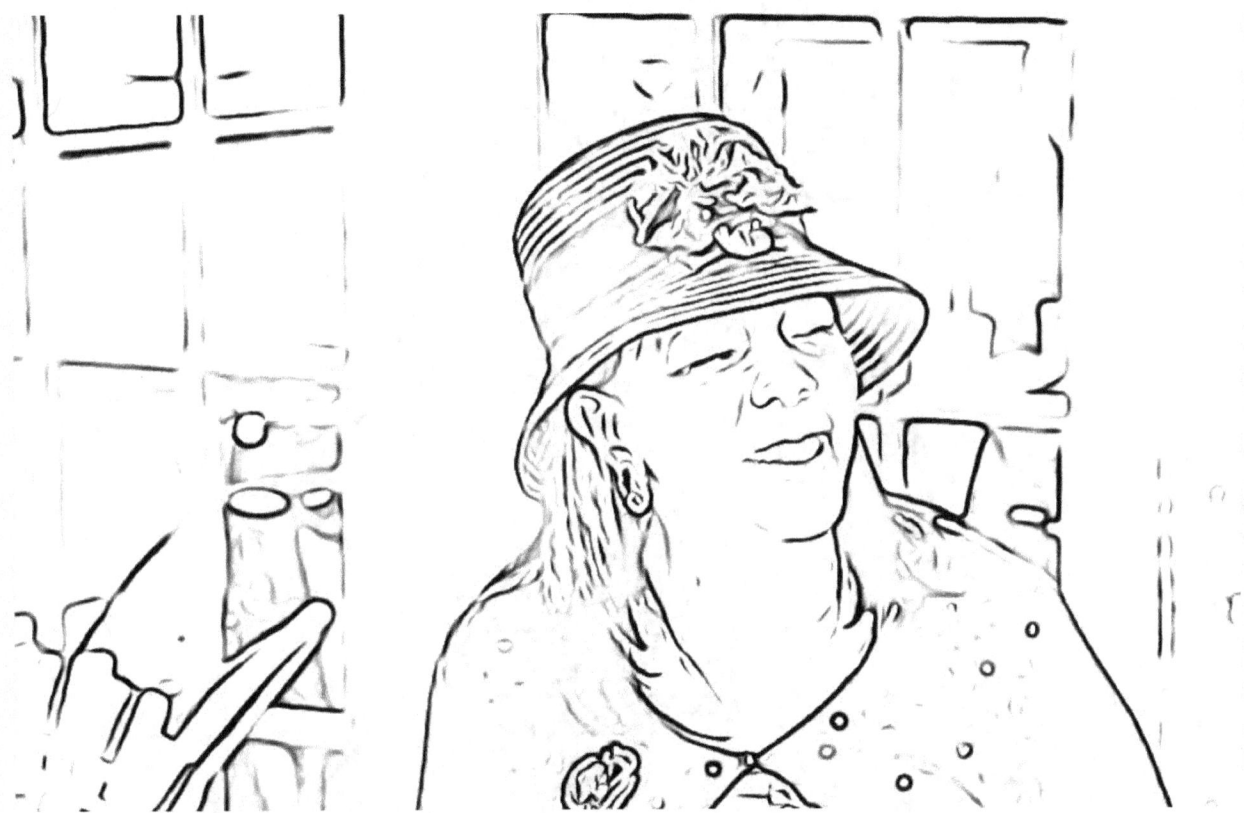

We work a lot so the grandparent, or mother in law steps in to watch the children. There is no schematic to family, we just embrace the help we do have and go from there.

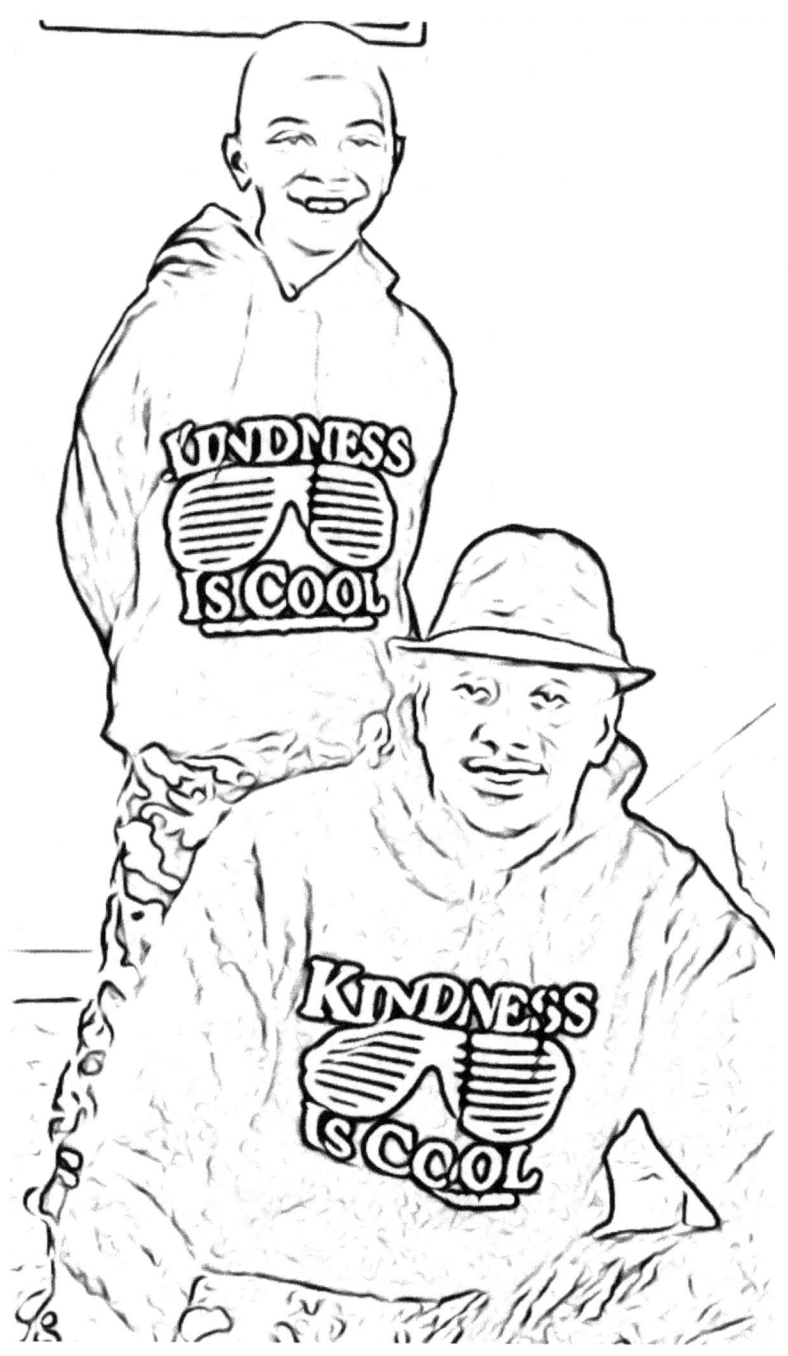

I have no idea how to impact my Son's life when he doesn't live with me. I just focus on the time being quality even though I want more (quantity) time as well.

Coloring The Blended Family
Richard Patterson III

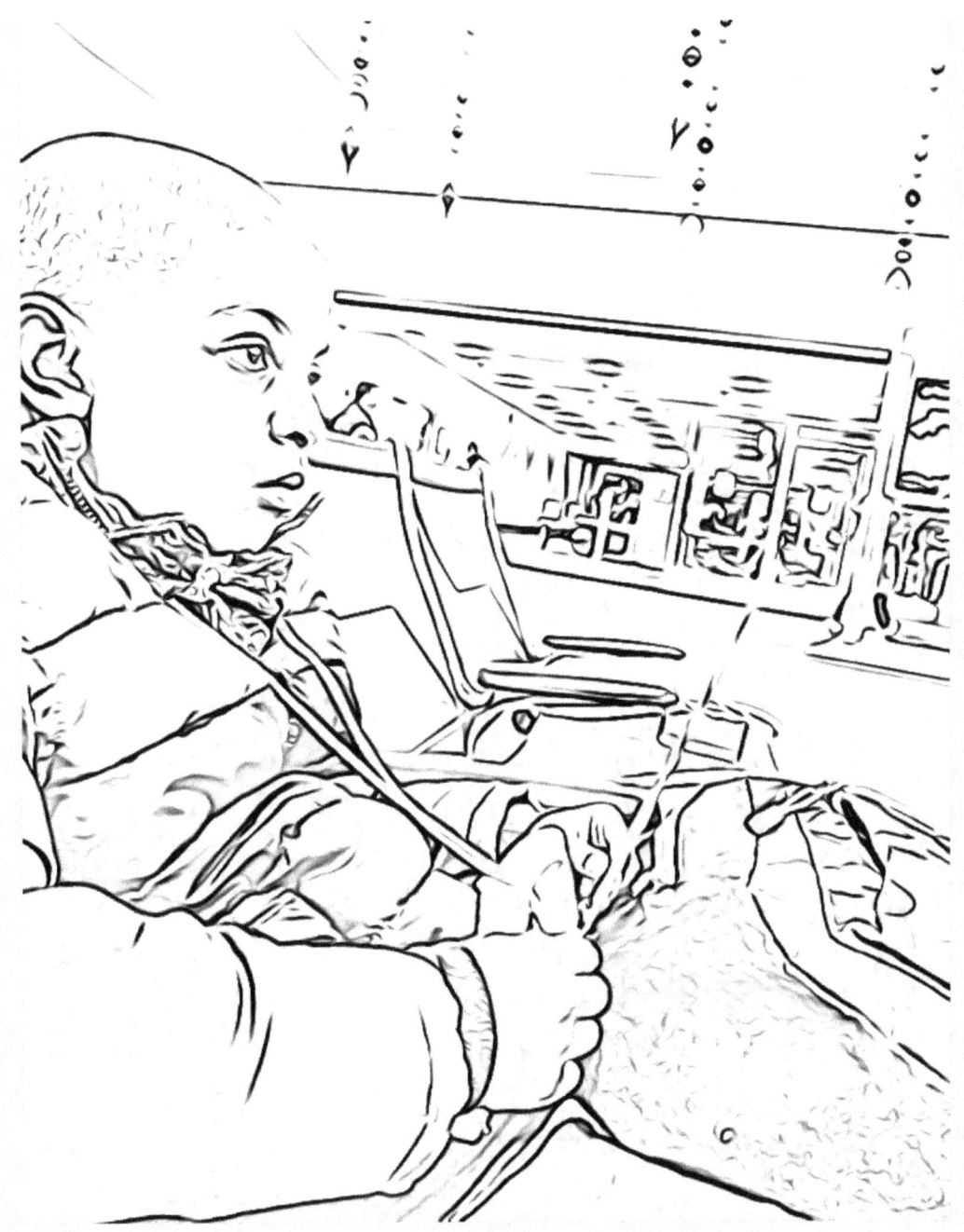

We wonder what our children see when they at themselves, but I'm just glad they have Family that allows them to understand who they are. We just have to trust the process and ask for help.

Coloring The Blended Family
Richard Patterson III

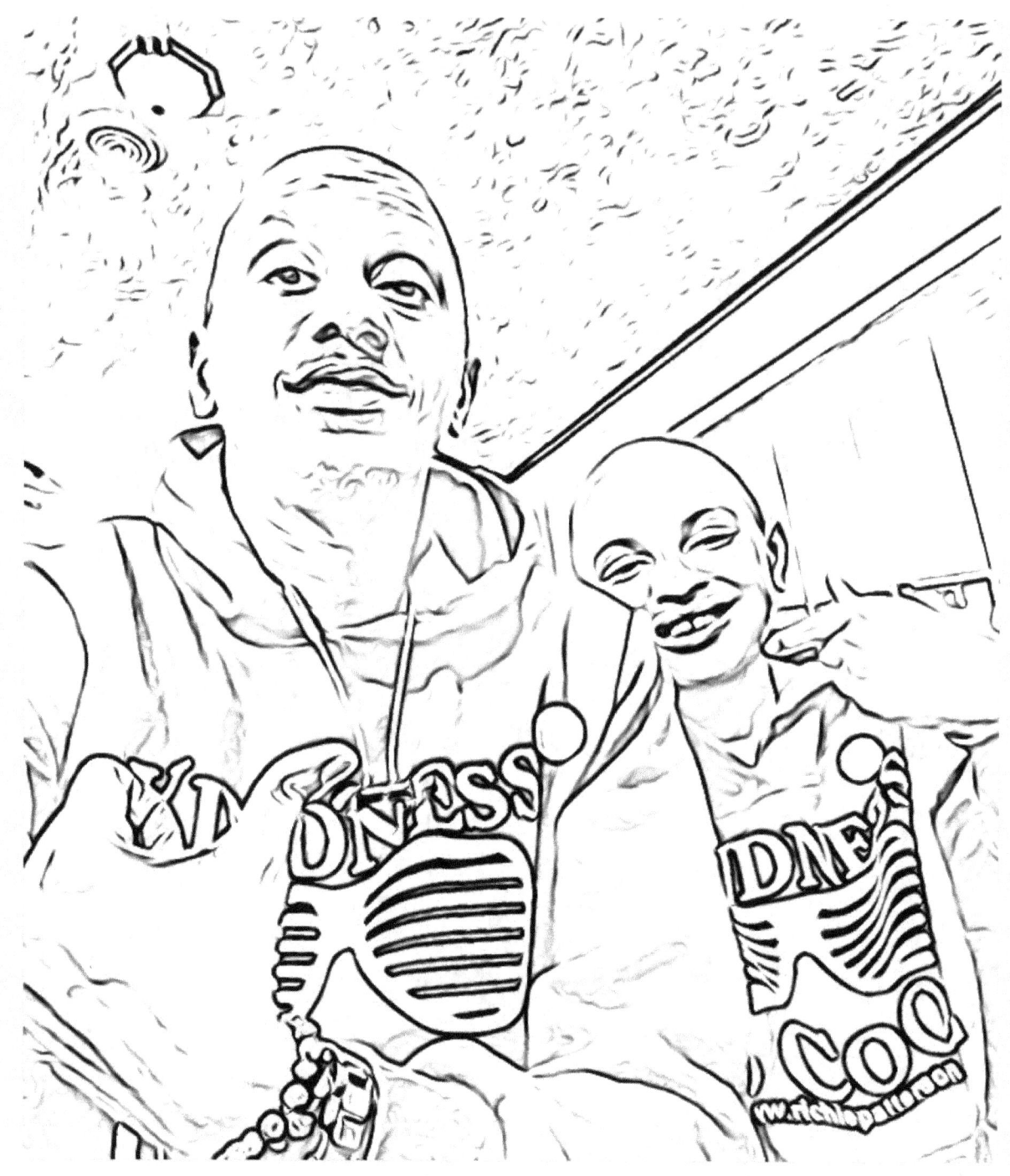

Parenting is not seasonal but it's a lifetime. How you start is not how you will finish. Make decisions with the future in mind and you'll have no regrets.

Coloring The Blended Family
Richard Patterson III

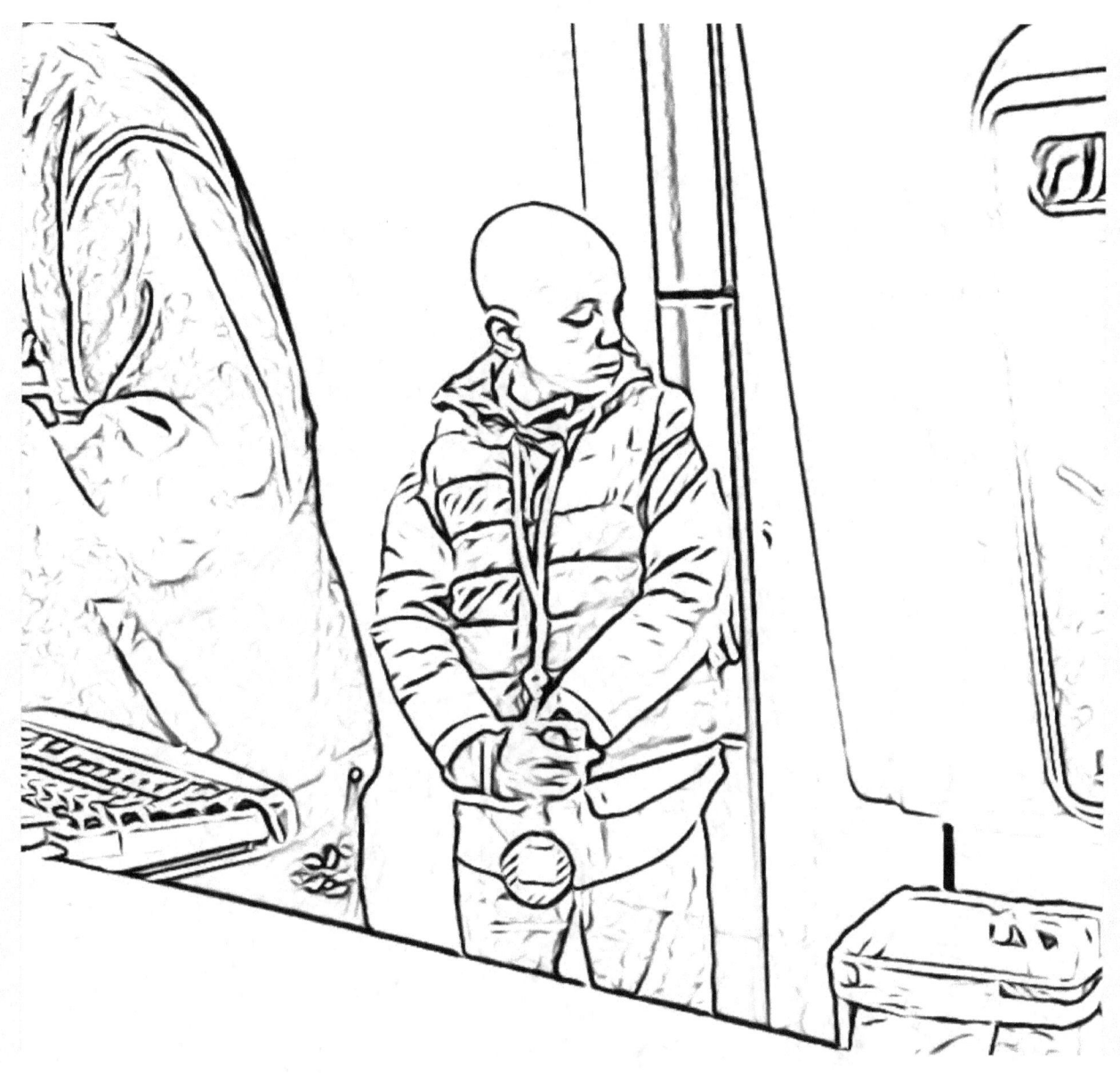

Identity comes from multiple sources, embrace all the help you can get. A son or a daughter will always be impacted by their community. Train them at home and expose them to people who mirror your values.

Coloring The Blended Family
Richard Patterson III

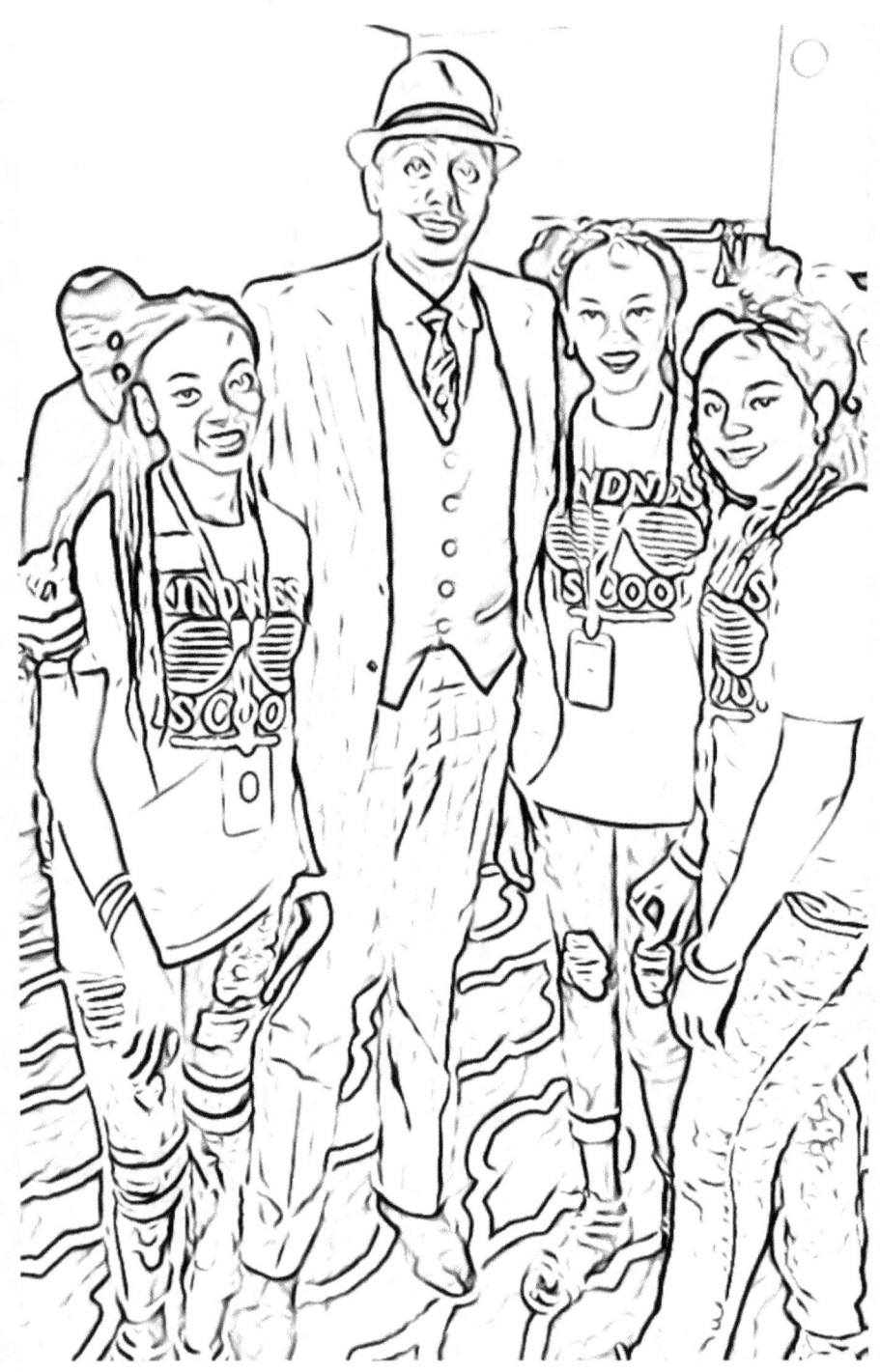

Cousins become Sisters because we spend so much time together. Blending is spending time with each other.

Coloring The Blended Family
Richard Patterson III

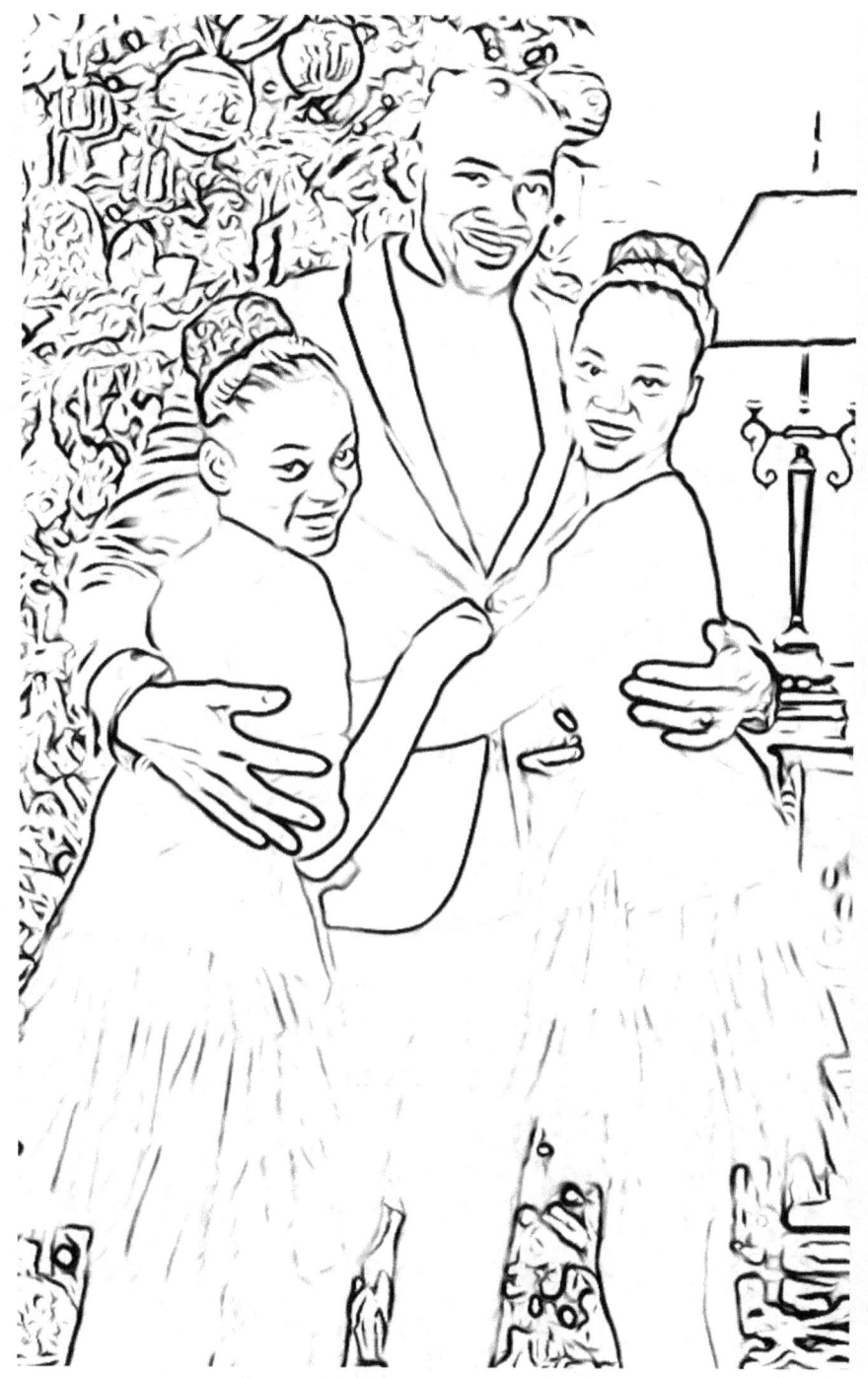

Someone's identity is being established because you continue to show up. Despite stereotypes and stigmas a "Good Parent" is as simple as being engaged with your time, support and affection.

Coloring The Blended Family
Richard Patterson III

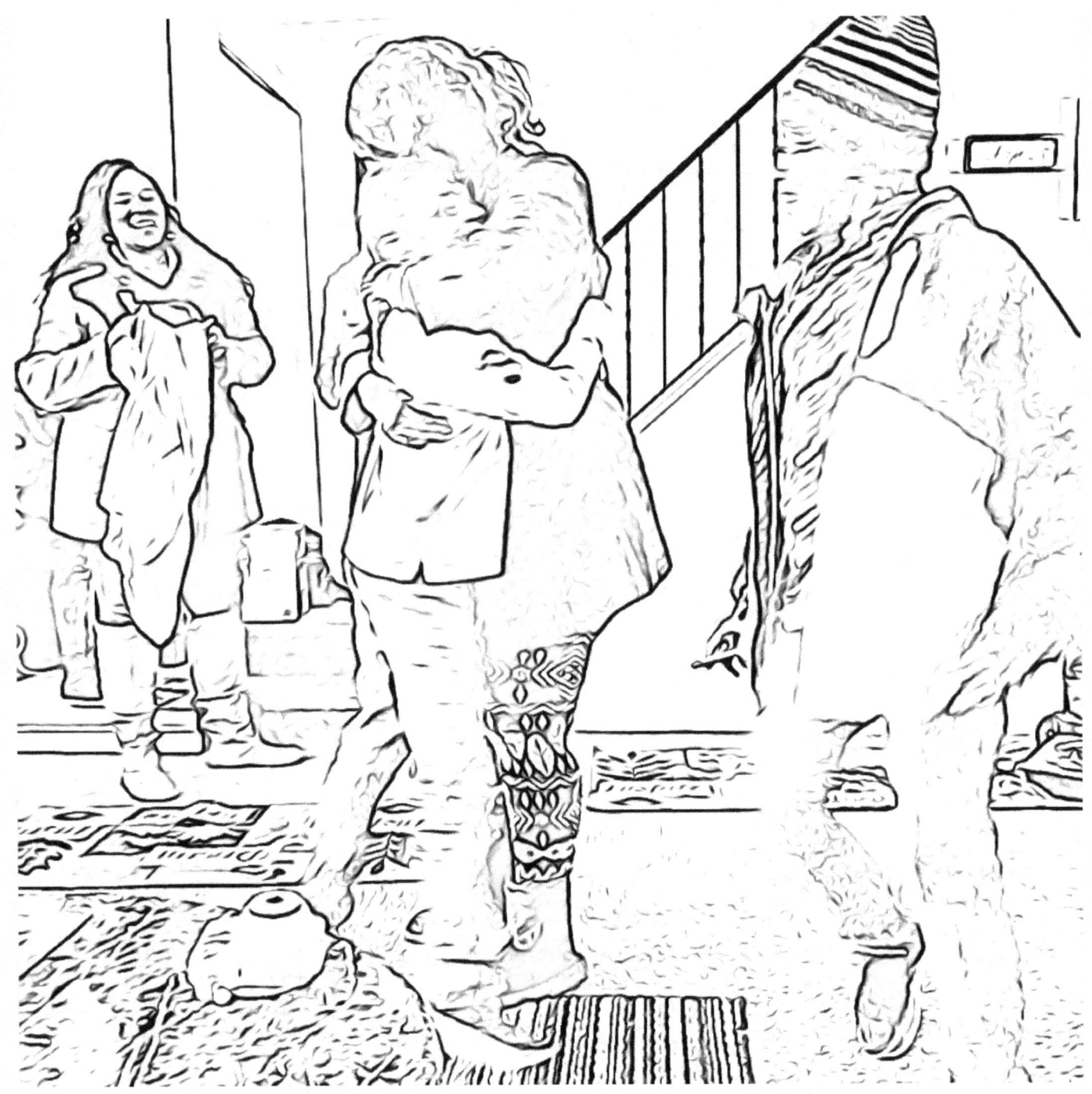

Love Blends us together. Love says maybe you were not there for the child in the past but let's see if we can work something out for their today and the future.

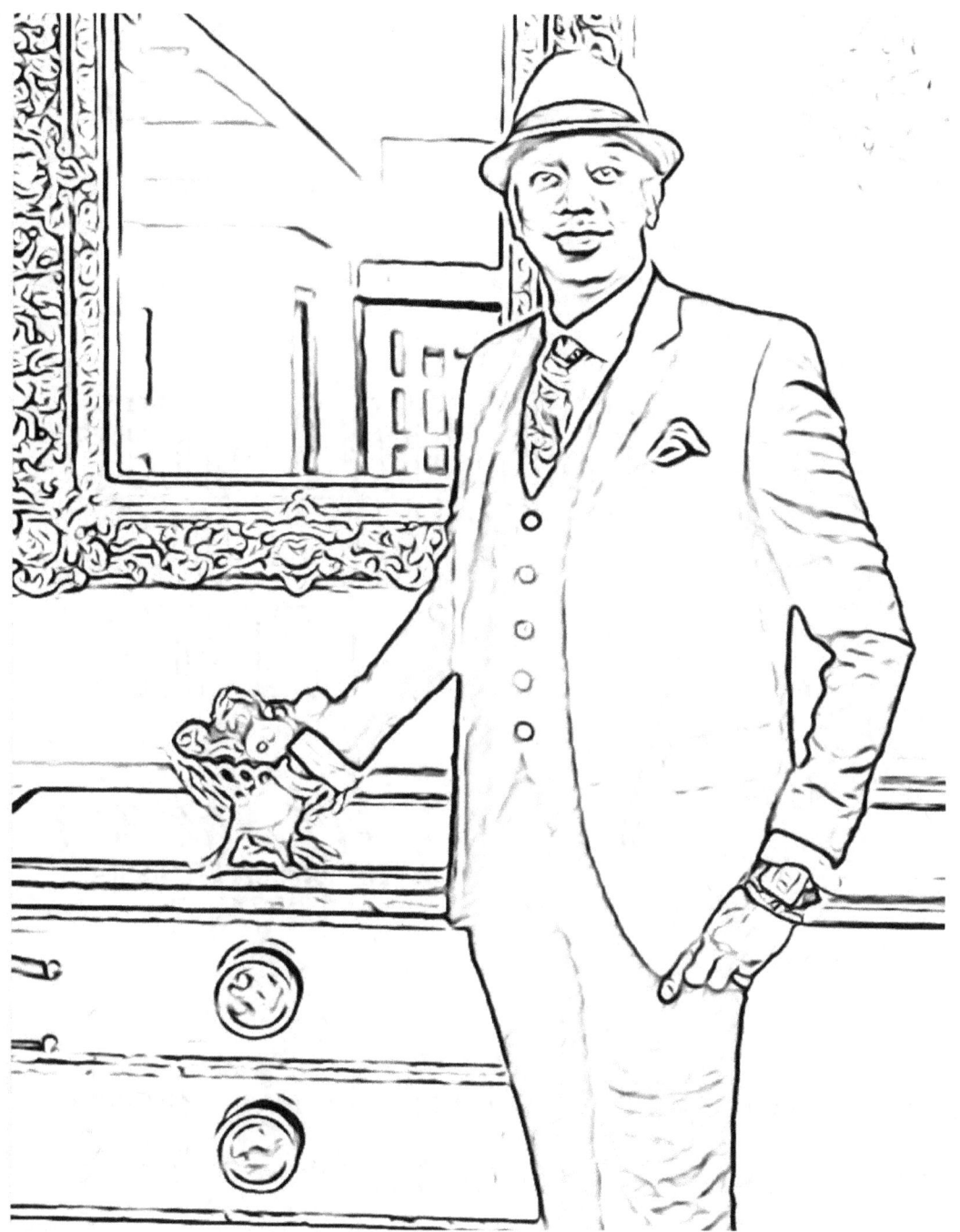

You may not be able to see a psychiatrist but in order for love to be the focus. You need a strong voice of reason that desires what's best for your family. Reaching out for help is not failure but that's how things get better.

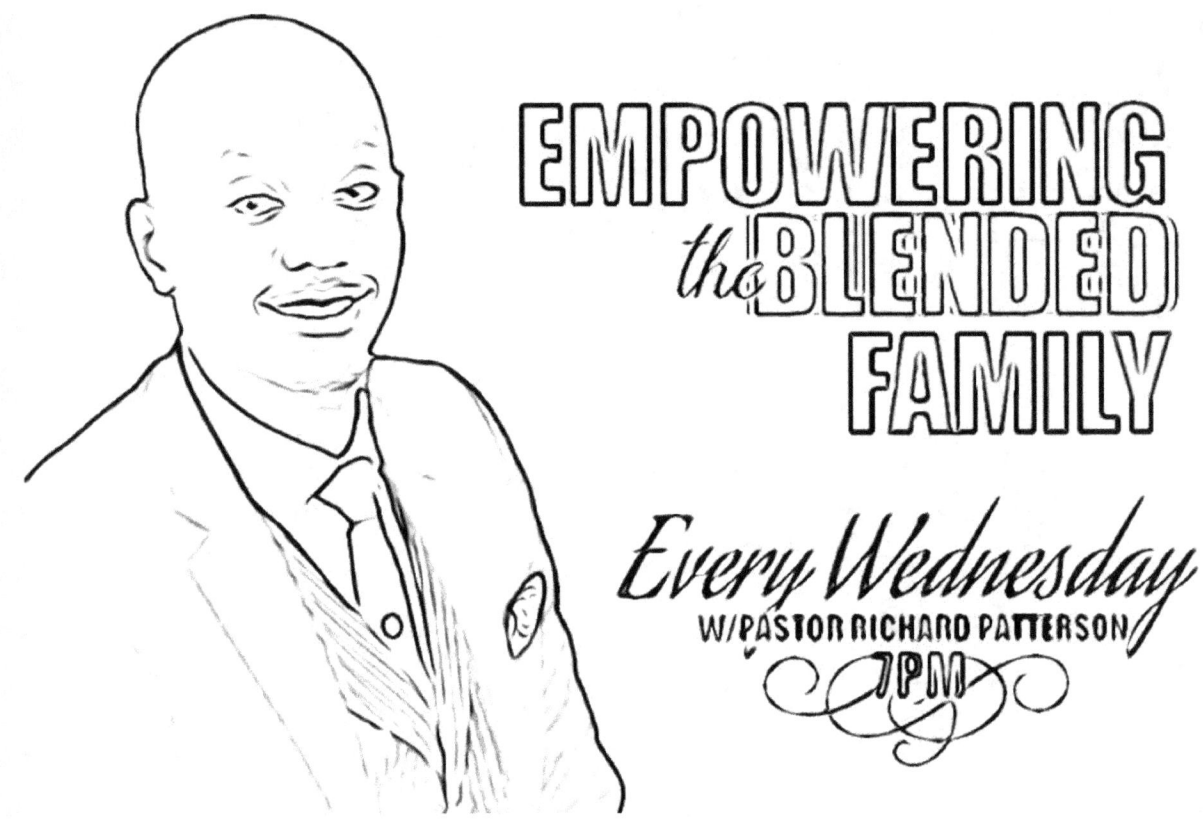

Empowering The Blended Family is a weekly open forum. Designed to give the parents, children and the entire family a way to rehearse the drama with us. So you don't have to live out the drama in your life. Skits, Role playing and table talk discussions weekly.

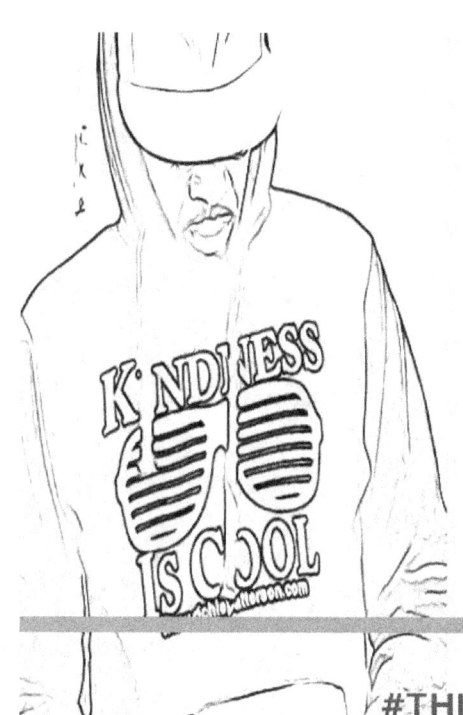

Empowering Fathers not degrading them Coloring The Blended Family

Cultivating creativity & family values through coloring
www.richiepatterson.com

#THISISTHEKINDNESS #COLORINGWITHKINDNESS

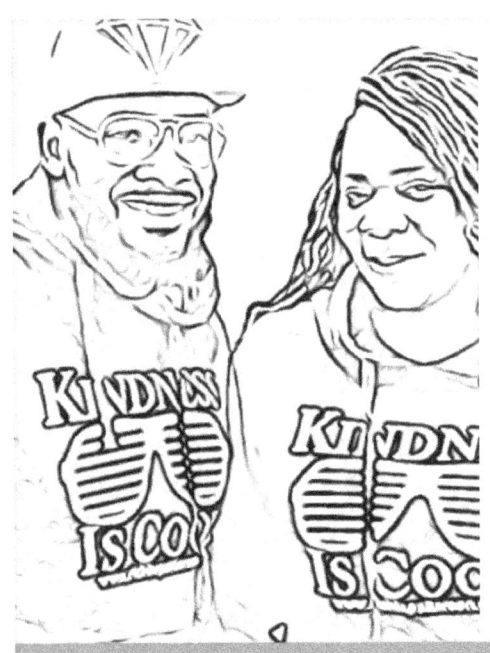

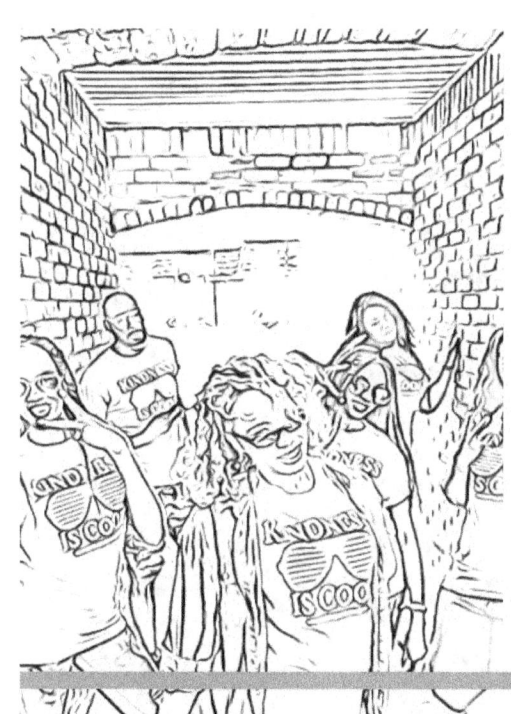

It takes a group effort to stop bullying Kindness is an approach not a reaction to bullying

Cultivating creativity & family values through coloring
www.richiepatterson.com

#THISISTHEKINDNESS #COLORINGWITHKINDNESS

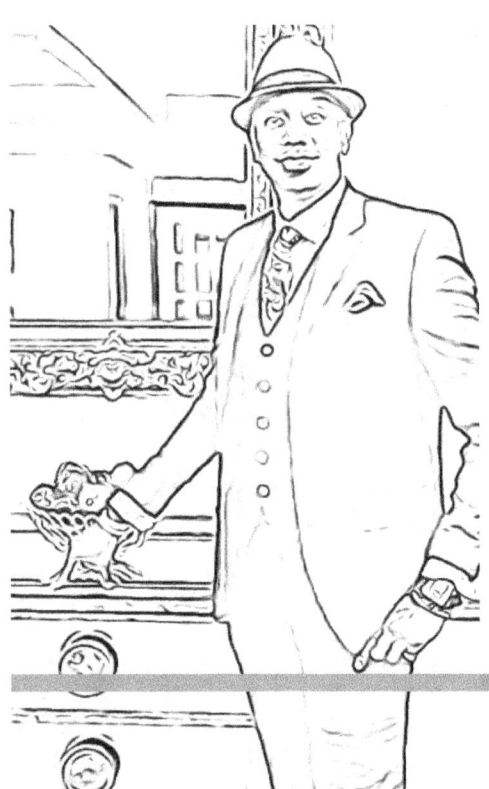

Available for Workshops, Speaking Engagements, Open Forums, Counseling Sessions And More

Pastor Richie Patterson III
8225 Allen Rd #1018
Allen Park, MI 48101
248.372.9500
www.richiepatterson.com

#THISISTHEKINDNESS
#COLORINGWITHKINDNESS

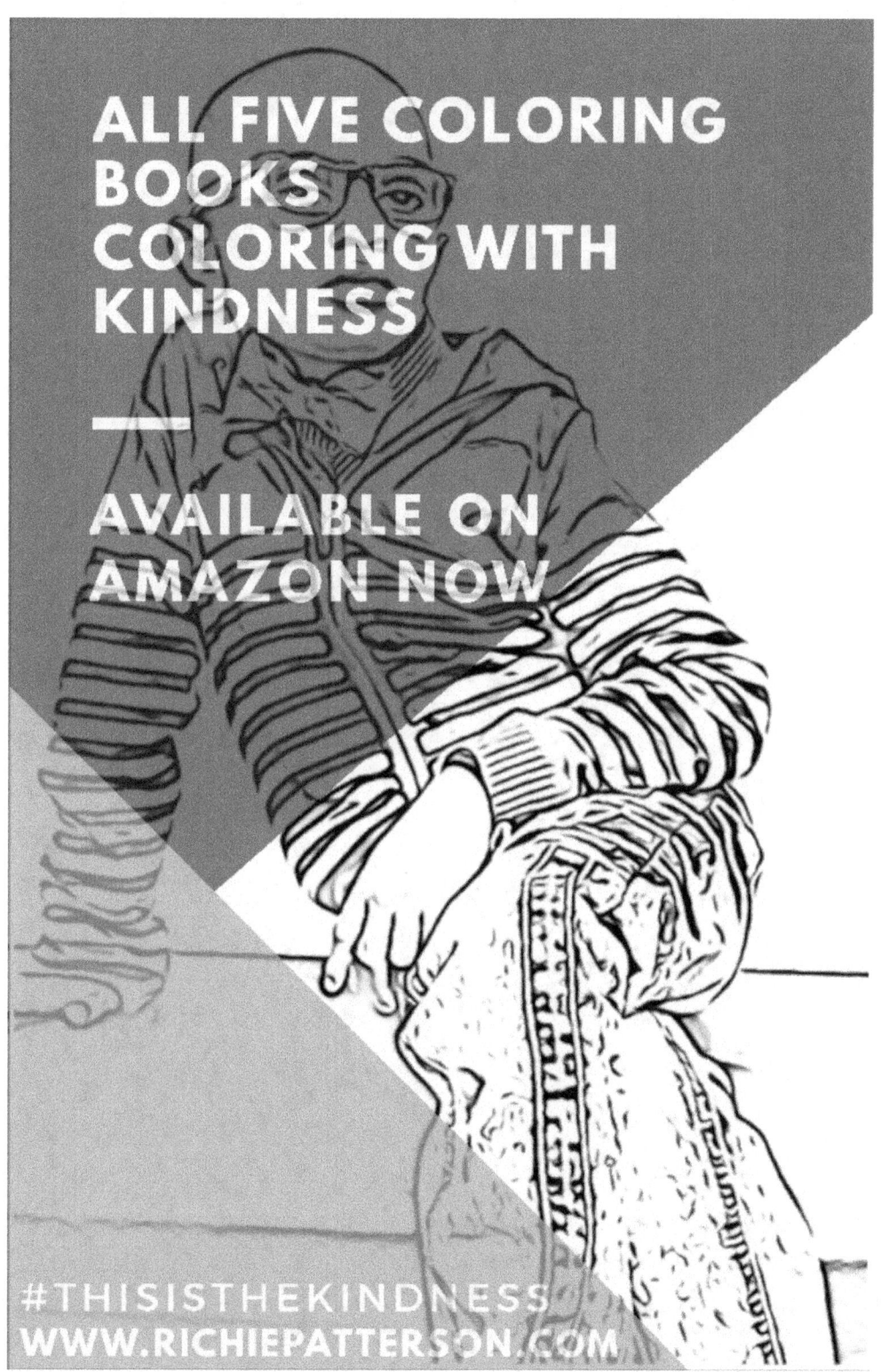

Coloring The Blended Family
Richard Patterson III

Coloring With Kindness, Page 36

Coloring The Blended Family
Richard Patterson III

Coloring The Blended Family
Richard Patterson III

Coloring With Kindness, Page 38

Coloring The Blended Family
Richard Patterson III

Coloring With Kindness , Page 39

Coloring The Blended Family
Richard Patterson III

Coloring The Blended Family
Richard Patterson III

Coloring The Blended Family
Richard Patterson III

Coloring With Kindness, Page 42

Coloring The Blended Family
Richard Patterson III

Coloring The Blended Family
Richard Patterson III

Coloring With Kindness, Page 44

Coloring The Blended Family
Richard Patterson III

Coloring With Kindness, Page 45

www.ingramcontent.com/pod-product-compliance
Lightning Source LLC
Chambersburg PA
CBHW062344220526
45469CB00008B/2829